Effective
Literacy
Coaching

Building Expertise and a Culture of Literacy

Shari Frost | Roberta Buhle | Camille Blachowicz

an ASCD
Action*TOOL*

COACH

COLLABORATE • DIRECT • CONTRIBUTE

Effective
Literacy
Coaching

Building Expertise and a Culture of Literacy

ASCD
LEARN. TEACH. LEAD.
Alexandria, Virginia USA

1703 North Beauregard St. • Alexandria, VA 22311-1714 USA
Phone: 1-800-933-2723 or 1-703-578-9600 • Fax: 1-703-575-5400
Web site: www.ascd.org • E-mail: member@ascd.org
Author guidelines: www.ascd.org/write

Gene R. Carter, *Executive Director*; Nancy Modrak, *Publisher*; Jennifer Barrett, *Content Development*; Mary Beth Nielsen, *Director, Editorial Services*; Alicia Goodman, *Project Manager*; Gary Bloom, *Director, Design and Production Services*; Greer Wymond, *Senior Graphic Designer*; Mike Kalyan, *Production Manager*; Carmen Yuhas, *Production Specialist*; Circle Graphics, *Desktop Publishing*

All Web links in this book are correct as of the publication date below but may have become inactive or otherwise modified since that time. If you notice a deactivated or changed link, please e-mail books@ascd.org with the words "Link Update" in the subject line. In your message, please specify the Web link, the book title, and the page number on which the link appears.

PAPERBACK ISBN: 978-1-4166-0850-9   ASCD Product #109044   n05/09

Quantity discounts for the paperback edition only: 10–49 copies, 10%; 50+ copies, 15%; for 1,000 or more copies, call 1-800-933-2723, ext. 5634, or 1-703-575-5634.

Library of Congress Cataloging-in-Publication Data
Frost, Shari, 1959-
    Effective literacy coaching: building expertise and a culture of literacy / Shari Frost, Roberta Buhle, Camille Blachowicz.
        p. cm.
    ISBN 978-1-4166-0850-9 (pbk. : alk. paper) 1. Language arts teachers—In-service training—United States. 2. Language arts—United States. 3. Individualized instruction—United States. I. Buhle, Roberta. II. Blachowicz, Camille L. Z. III. Association for Supervision and Curriculum Development. IV. Title.
    LB1576.F75 2009
    372.6'044—dc22

                                2009005399

16 15 14 13 12 11 10 09   1 2 3 4 5 6 7 8 9 10

Effective
Literacy •——— Coaching

Building Expertise and a Culture of Literacy

PART 1: THE COACH'S ROLE

PART 2: PROFESSIONAL DEVELOPMENT

Tools for Teacher Self-Evaluation

Tools for Assessment

Tools for Instruction

PART 3: LEADERSHIP FOR A SOLID INFRASTRUCTURE

Downloads

Electronic versions of the tools are available for download
at **www.ascd.org/downloads**.

Enter this unique key code to unlock the files:
G9439-0EFA4-0A415

If you have difficulty accessing the files, e-mail webhelp@ascd.org
or call 1-800-933-ASCD for assistance.

Acknowledgments

This book is dedicated to all the literacy coaches who are on the frontlines of a school's literacy accomplishments.

Just as coaching is a collaborative act, so too is learning and writing about coaching. We would like to acknowledge all our colleagues who have been so formative in our thinking and work:

- Our colleagues in Literacy Partners, National-Louis University's (NLU's) urban outreach project: Donna Ogle, Amy Correa, Ann Bates, Claudia Katz, Susan McMahon, Eileen Owens, Debbie Gurvitz, Barb Kaufman, Chris Seidman, Marcia Caulkins, Carrie Kamin Swann, and Pamela Pifer.
- Our partners in the Reading Leadership Institute, especially those from Evanston Skokie District 65, Ellen Fogelberg and Linda Shusterman and their team.
- Our colleagues in the Reading and Language Department at National-College of Education of NLU.
- The students in the Reading Program at NLU and the members of the Effective Literacy Coaching Class and the Literacy Coaching Collaborative who live this role every day.
- Our colleagues in the Chicago Public Schools, especially Barbara Eason-Watkins, Jodi Doddskinner and her team of literacy leaders, and Xavier Botana and his curriculum leaders; Jim Cosme; Carol Coughlin; Kelly Jeffers and all the literacy leaders and teachers in Area 6; and Javier Arriola and Donna Nelson and their faculty and staff at Rachel Carson and Murphy Schools, all of whom have done such a great job of moving coaching in a great urban school system forward.

- Peggy Mueller of the Chicago Community Trust and to the Searle Funds at the Chicago Community Trust for supporting the development of our work.
- The Shaw Fund for Literacy and the Michael W. Louis Fund for Literacy, both of which gave us the impetus and support to begin this work.
- To all the above, to the many other professionals with whom we work, and to our families for their patience, love, and support.

Shari Frost
Roberta Buhle
Camille Blachowicz

Introduction

Action tool is a perfect name for a resource for you, the literacy professional. Taking action is what you do every day with teachers, administrators, parents, and children. Part of your professional role is to make good decisions on a daily basis and be able to explain to others the foundation for that decision making, using evidence from both exemplary practice and research.

Aimed at the literacy professional for grades K–12, this action tool is designed to help you fulfill your responsibilities for developing and facilitating literacy curriculum and instruction and supporting teachers and administrators.

The reality-tested models and strategies in this action tool are founded on the components of the research-based Literacy Coaching Institute's coaching model. This model reflects that a coach needs to develop three areas of expertise: an understanding of the coaching role in school change, an understanding of the literacy process and how to

The Literacy Coaching
Institute's Coaching Model
_____

The Literacy Coaching Institute's Coaching Model

	Desired Outcomes	Role of the Coach
Literacy Instruction	• Rich literacy environments in school and classroom. • Well-organized and -managed literacy curriculum and instruction in school and classrooms. • Effective assessments and use of assessment data. • Differentiation of instruction. • Problem-solving approaches. • Improved student achievement.	• Help develop rich literacy environments at building and classroom levels. • Help develop, maintain, and manage well-organized literacy curriculum and instruction at the school and classroom levels. • Help develop, maintain, interpret, and use assessments and assessment data. • Support differentiated instruction. • Demonstrate, observe and/or team teach, guide, and problem solve in classrooms with teachers and students. • Stay connected to students and student learning by maintaining some direct interactions with students.
Professional Development	• Directed and organized professional development in literacy for teachers and administrators. • Professional communities of educators who engage in reflective practices and who problem solve around literacy. • Improved student achievement.	• Initiate, direct, and organize literacy professional development for teachers and administrators. • Develop personal and professional resources to promote self-analysis. • Help establish professional communities that reflect and problem solve around literacy. • Act as a resource for all members of the school community: students, teachers, administrators, parents, volunteers, and paraprofessionals. • Maintain a coaching schedule that is available and transparent to all staff.
Infrastructure	• Structures for developing, maintaining, and monitoring school literacy curriculum and practices. • Plans to support and sustain continuous improvement. • Regular, routine communication and problem solving about literacy and literacy decisions with administrators, teachers, parents, and district and state personnel. • Improved student achievement.	• Work with principals and teachers to develop plans needed to support and sustain continuous improvement in literacy. • Work with principals and teachers to build structures that develop, maintain, and monitor literacy curriculum and practices. • Ensure effective, regular communication and problem solving about literacy and literacy decisions with administrators, teachers, other school staff, parents, and district and state personnel. • Advocate for literacy in the school and community by spotlighting and celebrating achievement, innovations, and growth.

structure professional development for excellence, and an understanding of the infrastructure a school needs for exemplary literacy instruction. These areas have helped us develop the tools that follow, and you can use the model as a handy reference for organizing your thinking. Within each of the areas, the literacy coach has myriad outcomes, roles, essential knowledge, and essential literacy practices to support.

If you are not familiar with the characteristics of a balanced reading program, we recommend that you consult some of the many published examples of balanced programs, such

Essential Knowledge for Coaches	Essential Literacy Practices for Coaches to Support
• Conducive climates for literacy learning. • How readers and writers develop. • The nature and structure of developmental reading programs. • The nature of sequenced, cohesive, and balanced literacy curriculum. • Research-based methods of instruction and differentiation. • Organization of literacy materials at the classroom and school levels. • Appropriate formative and summative assessments. • Instructional problem-solving strategies.	• Flexible grouping to differentiate instruction. • Implementation of instructional strategies for writing, vocabulary development, comprehension, independent-level reading, word study, inquiry learning, literature circles, guided reading, and read-alouds. • Administration and interpretation of assessments for planning, instruction, problem solving, and progress monitoring. • The intelligent and selective use of published materials and other instructional resources.
• Forms of adult learning styles and modalities, and how to develop a professional voice. • Ways to encourage discussion. • Research on professional collaborations. • Trust-building and problem-solving strategies. • How to build collaborative learning communities. • An understanding of self-inquiry and how to plan for one's own professional development.	• Differentiated professional development. • Study groups and book clubs. • Grade-level and building-level literacy team meetings. • Development and use of laboratory classrooms. • Opening and maintenance of a literacy resource center. • Ongoing maintenance of a professional library. • Collection of local samples of best practice in the form of student work, videos, and resources. • Communication of professional development opportunities. • Networking and professional memberships.
• Research on the nature of change and school-change models. • School planning processes for literacy. • Ways to conduct a needs analysis. • How to develop literacy curriculum. • Modes of communicating. • The power of motivation and engagement. • How to implement backward and forward planning.	• Assessment of school literacy needs and the evaluation of progress. • Development of a school plan for literacy. • Integration of district mandates with local needs. • Development of a model to sustain literacy growth. • Routine scheduled meetings with administration, teachers, grade levels, and so forth. • Organization of district and local assessment for analysis and effective use. • Maintenance of all building literacy records to facilitate future actions. • Evaluation of school literacy progress.

as those found in the work of Linda Dorn, Lucy Calkins, and Irene Fountas and Gay Su Pinnell. Our concept of balance for upper-level students is well expressed in *Reading Comprehension: Strategies for Independent Learners* (Blachowicz & Ogle, 2008), which provided the underpinnings for some of our grade 6–12 strategies.

Reference

Blachowicz, C., & Ogle, D. (2008). *Reading comprehension: Strategies for independent learners* (2nd ed.). New York: Guilford Press.

Organization of This Action Tool

The tools in this guide are organized according to the Literacy Coaching Institute's coaching model that groups the literacy coach's responsibilities within the school community, professional organizations, and university partnerships into three overlapping spheres:

- Collaborate for excellence in literacy instruction.
- Direct professional development.
- Contribute to an effective infrastructure for literacy.

The tools in Part 1 are reflection activities that an individual coach or the curriculum or coaching director can use to define goals and roles. They focus on your personal development as a literacy professional and understanding coaching and literacy facilitation. This part includes exercises to help you understand the process of school change and the role the coach plays in this process. It also shares strategies for working with adult learners, setting goals for change, and building a job description and schedule to help you get things done. At the beginning of the section, the comprehensive Literacy Coaching Institute's Coach's Self-Evaluation will help you set goals for your learning and work.

The tools in parts 2 and 3 are targeted for coaches to use when working with teachers, administrators, and parents. These sections task literary coaches to ask teachers standard probing questions—such as "Why do you say that?", "What might you change?", and "What could you do about this?"—to help teachers evaluate their own levels of conceptual or pedagogical knowledge.

The tools in Part 2 deal with becoming a professional development expert for literacy within the school. This section includes such topics as communicating and setting literacy goals; setting up a literacy classroom, literacy schedule, and literary closet; using assessment to inform instruction; and selecting materials and enacting the curriculum.

Part 3 focuses on building the school infrastructure for literacy, building teams to get things done, and leading self-study. In addition, it offers ideas for opening and maintaining lines of communication within and outside of the school.

ELECTRONIC TOOLS AND RESOURCES

Interactive versions of the tools are available for download. To access these documents, visit www.ascd.org/downloads and enter the key code found on page viii. All files are saved in Adobe Portable Document Format (PDF). The PDF is compatible with both personal computers (PCs) and Macintosh computers. **Note: You must have the Adobe Acrobat Professional software on your machine to save your work.** The main menu will let you navigate through the various sections, and you can print individual tools or sections in their entirety. If you are having difficulties downloading or viewing the files, contact webhelp@ascd.org for assistance, or call 1-800-933-ASCD.

Minimum System Requirements

Program: The most current version of the Adobe Reader software is available for free download at www.adobe.com.

PC: Intel Pentium Processor; Microsoft Windows XP Professional or Home Edition (Service Pack 1 or 2), Windows 2000 (Service Pack 2), Windows XP Tablet PC Edition, Windows Server 2003, or Windows NT (Service Pack 6 or 6a); 128 MB of RAM (256 MB recommended); up to 90 MB of available hard-disk space; Internet Explorer 5.5 (or higher), Netscape 7.1 (or higher), Firefox 1.0, or Mozilla 1.7.

Macintosh: PowerPC G3, G4, or G5 processor, Mac OS X v.10.2.8–10.3; 128 MB of RAM (256 MB recommended); up to 110 MB of available hard-disk space; Safari 1.2.2 browser supported for MAC OS X 10.3 or higher.

Getting Started

Select "Download files." Designate a location on your computer to save the zip file. Choose to open the PDF file with your existing version of Adobe Acrobat Reader, or install the newest version of Adobe Acrobat Reader from www.adobe.com. From the main menu, select a section by clicking on its title. To view a specific tool, open the Bookmarks tab in the left navigation pane and then click on the title of the tool.

Entering and Saving Text

To enter text on the form, position your cursor inside a form field and click. The pointer will change to an I-beam to allow you to enter text. If the pointer changes to a pointing finger, you can select a check box or radio button. Press Enter or Return to create a paragraph return in the field. Press the Tab key or use your mouse to move between fields. To cancel an entry, press the Escape button to restore the previous text or to deselect a field. **Remember, you must have Adobe Acrobat Professional to save your work.**

Printing Tools

To print a single tool, select the tool by clicking on its title via the Bookmarks section and the printer icon, or select File then Print. In the Print Range section, select Current Page to print the page on the screen. To print several tools, enter the page range in the "Pages from" field. If you wish to print all of the tools in the section, select All in the Printer Range section and then click OK.

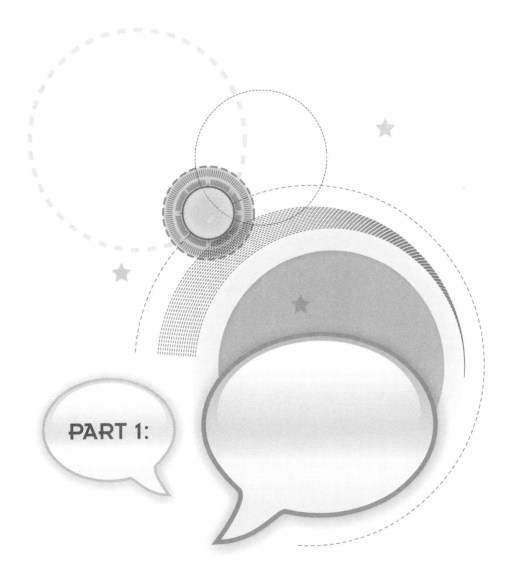

PART 1:

The Coach's Role

Coach's Self-Evaluation

TARGET
Elementary ✓   Middle School/High School ✓

Literacy coaches strive to build a quality literacy program, but what exactly does a quality literacy program entail? Literacy program experts have devised a list of the nine basic characteristics of an effective program.

Matthew Hanson, Lizanne DeStefano, Peggy Mueller, and Barbara Eason-Watkins (2006) provide a global structure for looking at systemic indicators of change in "9 Indicators of High Performance in School Literacy Improvement." In conjunction with information from Linda Dorn's workshops "Comprehensive K–12 Literacy Model for School Change," the following characteristics of a quality literacy program emerge:

1. rich literacy environment
2. well-organized and well-managed literacy instruction
3. use of assessment data
4. differentiated instruction
5. coaching
6. professional development
7. reflective practice
8. shared vision
9. advocacy

Administration, the faculty, and other school personnel are responsible for fostering and developing these characteristics, and the literacy coach can spearhead this effort. The first step is to determine the status of the school's existing literacy program. Then you can work with other stakeholders to create a plan to effect change in areas of need across the school.

References for further learning

DeStefano, E., Hanson, M., & Kallemeyn, L. (2005). *Evaluation report of the Advanced Reading Development Demonstration Project: Year three report to the Chicago Community Trust.* Urbana-Champaign: University of Illinois.

Hanson, M. R., DeStefano, L., Mueller, P., & Eason-Watkins, B. (2006, April). Development, validation, and use of "The indicators of high literacy performance": A framework for improving school literacy programs. In William F. Tate (Chair), *Education research in the public interest.* Symposium conducted at the meeting of the American Educational Research Association, San Francisco, CA.

GOAL

- To determine the status of the school's existing literacy program.

IMPLEMENTATION

1. Rate your school's literacy program in terms of the characteristics on the Literacy Coach Self-Evaluation Rating Guide.
2. Record the scores on the Coaching Worksheet.
3. Once you've determined where your institute stands, use the worksheet to brainstorm ways that you can make changes to improve your rating in these important areas.
4. You can also use the evaluation as a starting point for conversations with the principal (see "Communicating with the Principal" on page 177).

REFLECTION, EVALUATION, AND PLANNING

1. Do you see a correlation between areas with high ratings? How about between areas with low ratings? How would making changes in one area affect another characteristic?
2. What resources can you tap to help plan and execute change in the school?
3. Which characteristics should you focus on first? Is there any one area that needs more immediate help?
4. Can you set time lines for reaching your goals?

Literacy Coach Self-Evaluation Rating Guide

Characteristic 1: Rich Literacy Environment

The environment exhibits:

- The availability of a variety of appropriate, accessible materials in both classroom and libraries.
- Classroom libraries.
- Well-organized classroom space.
- Displays of student work in classrooms and across the school.
- Reflections of integrated curriculum.
- Evidence of attention to motivated instructional design.
- Student engagement and sharing of reading, writing, listening, and speaking activities.
- Students reading and writing, including informational and personal reading.
- Positive and respectful teacher-child interactions.
- Parent involvement and communication.
- Positive and collaborative teacher and administrator attitudes toward the curriculum and students.

Rating

1—Not Evident	Impoverished environment. Uninspired, teacher-directed instruction. Limited instructional materials. Books not accessible to students. Formal or punitive teacher-child interactions. Few displays of student work. Student work formulaic, fill-in. Teachers unable to articulate a coherent philosophy. Literacy time inadequate or interrupted.
2—Basic	Classroom library is being developed. Appropriate core instructional materials. Meaningful student work displayed. Respectful classroom environment. Teacher conscious of the need for motivation. Students observed in reading and writing, including personal reading. Teacher can articulate a basic philosophy. Adequate time for literacy.
3—Established	Extensive classroom library, including periodicals and informational materials. Varied and appropriate instructional materials. Some integration of curriculum. Instruction includes dialogue and student constructive activity. Some evidence of student inquiry. Teacher can articulate a broad philosophy of literacy. Student work evident and meaningful. Adequate time for literacy.
4—Exemplary	All characteristics of "Established" in addition to literacy permeating the classroom and school environment as a cross-curricular responsibility. Inquiry learning is evident along with integration of instruction. Teachers can articulate an explicit philosophy of literacy, and students can articulate relevant literacy beliefs and understandings.

Characteristic 2: Well-Organized and Well-Managed Literacy Instruction

Adequate, uninterrupted time is devoted to literacy, and this time is organized to maximize its effect. Teachers are aware of the diverse needs of students and respond to this diversity by selecting appropriate materials; working with whole-class, large, and small groups; and providing centers for independent practice and self-regulated learning. The classroom schedule reflects knowledge of the essential elements of a balanced and comprehensive literacy curriculum. There are reading, writing, speaking, and listening opportunities throughout the school day and curriculum. Students are aware of classroom routines and standards of behavior, and they exhibit both choice and responsibility in their literacy practices.

Rating

1—Not Evident	No regular schedule. Classrooms are poorly managed with materials scattered or sparse. Children are not on task. Noise level is distracting or rule of silence isn't enforced. Grouping is haphazard or whole group.
2—Basic	Instruction is primarily as a whole group with some small-group work. Meeting of needs is inconsistent. Range of reading materials is available, and children do some independent work in literacy centers. Children are aware of classroom standards and some routines but need reminders for behavior control.
3—Established	Well-organized classroom with appropriate materials to meet needs of diverse students. Teachers focus instruction on comprehension and problem solving, while continuing to meet the more basic needs of students. Flexible groups are evident. Students understand the class standards of behavior and are able to work independently on self-regulated or extension activities.
4—Exemplary	All characteristics of "Established" in addition to classrooms operating smoothly and efficiently with students showing that they have internalized the standards and routines of the class and can direct self-regulated learning. Students and teacher exhibit ability to reflect on their own learning.

Characteristic 3: Use of Assessment Data

Teachers and other literacy team members understand how to use data to inform and monitor instruction. They are capable administrators of classroom assessments and interpreters of formal district data.

Rating

1—Not Evident	Students are assessed with formal or other mandated assessments, but data are not used to group or monitor students. Progress monitoring does not take place.
2—Basic	Students are assessed with varied assessments, and data are used to group but data are not used to monitor students and instruction on a regular basis. Some problem solving does take place, but it is not ongoing or systematic within classroom or school.
3—Established	Students are assessed with varied assessment, including teacher-administered assessments, and data are used to group and monitor progress over time. Teachers collaboratively examine data and use it to plan reading and writing assessment as well as to problem solve about students who are not making progress.
4—Exemplary	All the characteristics of "Established" in addition to data being used to study patterns of achievement across the school and to make decisions about interventions and special support.

Characteristic 4: Differentiated Instruction

Teachers and other literacy team members understand how to provide differentiated instruction within a coherent literacy curriculum that includes options such as inquiry models, the workshop approach, project-based learning, and other models that develop self-regulated learning.

Rating

1—Not Evident	All instruction is whole group with the same textbook.
2—Basic	Some evidence of differentiation of materials, instruction, and performance but these seem to be more of an add-on to the general instruction of the class.
3—Established	Differentiation of materials, instruction, and performance are integral to the way instruction is organized and implemented and includes options such as inquiry models, the workshop approach, project-based learning, and other models that develop self-regulated learning.
4—Exemplary	All the characteristics of "Established" in addition to teachers being able to articulate theory of differentiation that enables them to make effective decisions within options for self-regulated learning.

Characteristic 5: Coaching

The school has a qualified reading specialist, coach, or lead literacy teacher who uses different approaches to coaching and mentoring and is available to school personnel and understands the need to differentiate for teachers.

Rating

1—Not Evident	No coaching.
2—Basic	Predetermined modules of coaching supplied; for example, how to do a DR-TA via modeling. Coach may be experienced but not highly qualified.
3—Established	Coaching by a highly qualified coach. Coaching differentiates and scaffolds appropriately for the needs of different teachers and includes modeling, teacher-supported practice, and teacher independent practice with feedback and discussion at each step.
4—Exemplary	All the characteristics of "Established" along with reflection by the teacher and sharing with other teachers.

Characteristic 6: Professional Development

The school community understands the importance of on-site, school-embedded professional development. Professional development is provided using a model that supports teacher learning and involves teachers in planning, implementing, and sharing their own work. Teachers take advantage of appropriate communication and sharing tools. Teachers also exhibit awareness of the larger professional community development activities can provide.

Rating

1—Not Evident	No embedded professional development.
2—Basic	On-site professional development coordinated with school goals.
3—Established	On-site professional development coordinated with school goals that involve teacher trials, sharing, and reflection. Teachers can use electronic tools for growth and communication and participate in local professional literacy organizations.
4—Exemplary	On-site professional development is coordinated with school goals that involve teacher trials, sharing, and reflection that leads to collaborative planning and execution of future professional development and sharing across schools. Teachers can use electronic tools for growth and communication and participate in local professional literacy organizations with some taking leadership in these groups.

Characteristic 7: Reflective Practice

The school community understands the need for self-reflection as a tool for professional development.

Rating

1—Not Evident	No evidence of self-reflection practices.
2—Basic	Literacy coaches use reflection logs daily, and some teachers use these in team meetings.
3—Established	Literacy coaches use reflection logs daily with evidence of deep thinking, including analysis and reflection of changes in classroom practices and student learning. Teachers are using these more regularly in team meetings as well as for deeper understanding of their work.
4—Exemplary	Literacy coaches and teachers use reflection logs as a basis for discussing teaching, students, curriculum, and professional development. New teachers are acculturated into the process by veteran teachers.

Characteristic 8: Shared Vision

The school community understands the importance of a shared, schoolwide literacy vision with a well-articulated vision for planning, initiating, monitoring, and assessing change and growth over time.

Rating

1—Not Evident	No consistent assessment and instruction across grades and classrooms. Lack of articulation across grades and with special and supplemental teachers. No sense of past or future direction.
2—Basic	A literacy plan has been developed and approved by the school staff. Short-term and long-term goals are in place. There is consistency within a grade and an awareness of total school literacy curriculum and initiatives.
3—Established	The school literacy plan is used to assess teacher performance and change and student achievement. There is a well-articulated transition across grades, as well as consistency within grades and with supplemental and special teachers. Teachers understand the literacy plan, goals, and appropriate benchmarks for measuring change over time.
4—Exemplary	All the characteristics of "Established" in addition to the plan being embedded across the curriculum.

Characteristic 9: Advocacy

The school community understands the importance of advocating for literacy and spotlights the school literacy program in a positive and professional way.

Rating

1—Not Evident	Negative attitudes and lack of commitment to the school literacy program and students' learning.
2—Basic	A professional and collaborative attitude is exhibited about the school's literacy program. There is a shared belief that students can learn to read.
3—Established	There is a plan to advocate for and spotlight the school's literacy program. The program is shared with school boards, teacher groups, parents, and other interested stakeholders.
4—Exemplary	All the characteristics of "Established" in addition to the school's program being shared with other schools, systems, and the wider public through presentation, publication, and by other means.

Coaching Worksheet

Characteristic	Where my school is with respect to this characteristic	What we need/need to do to make progress
1. Rich literacy environment		
2. Well-organized and well-managed literacy instruction		
3. Use of assessment		
4. Differentiated instruction		
5. Coaching		
6. Professional development		
7. Reflective practice		
8. Shared vision		
9. Advocacy		

Making the Best Use of Your Time

TARGET
Elementary ✓   Middle School/High School ✓

Reading specialists have long been a valuable staple in schools, but the literacy coaching position is frequently considered the new kid on the block—even if the literacy coach was the former reading specialist in the building. Reading specialists were seen as important resources for teachers and principals but spent most of their time working with students. In contrast, literacy coaches, as they are defined here, spend most of their time working directly with teachers in small groups, large groups, and one-on-one.

Because of this shift in their role, many of today's coaches struggle to find ways to spend their time so that they will make a difference. If literacy coaches want change to take place, they have to arrange a schedule that allows for it to happen.

Some coaches perform clerical duties, such as ordering materials, organizing books in the school's literacy closet (see "Organizing a Literacy Closet" on page 208), and entering data into computers. Others perform duties that could be seen as administrative, such as organizing how testing will be done. Still others see themselves as liaisons to the community, organizing family reading nights (see "Planning a Family Reading Night" on page 221) and working with libraries.

There will never be a perfect distribution of coaching time, but the bottom line for most districts, school administrators, teachers, and coaches is that they want literacy coaches to make a difference in their students' literacy. They know that requires coaches to work intensively with teachers to improve their learning, their knowledge, and their practice. As a result, today's coaches must constantly reflect on whether the way they use their time reflects this goal.

The following Literacy Coach Activities Pie Chart can reveal how you currently divide your time. At a deeper level, it reflects what the school currently asks of you, which may not be in line with what the school really wants the literacy coach to do. If what is asked

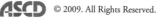

of you diverges from the bottom line, you can share the form with administrators and with teachers to spark conversation about whether your responsibilities reflect their expectations. The tool can also serve as a springboard to develop short- and long-term action plans to change the coach's role.

GOALS

- To develop a set of priorities for how the literacy coach's time is spent.
- To serve as a starting point for conversations with administration and staff regarding the role of a literacy coach in their building.
- To help plan short- and long-term plans to change the coach's role.

IMPLEMENTATION

1. Decide whether the chart will represent a day or a week. Choose whichever suits your work best.
2. Pick a period of the school year that best represents your work, avoiding the beginning or end of school when special activities, such as testing, occur.
3. Make a list of all the activities you usually perform during the selected time. You can refer to lesson plans to help you account for your time, but if they frequently change, let your circle reflect reality.
4. Divide and label pie-shaped sections of the circle to show percentages of time typically spent in each activity. Do not include time outside the school day, even if you are paid for it. The result should document a typical school day or week, including the short period of time before and after school when all teachers are required to be present. Among other activities, you will likely include the items below:

   - in classrooms, supporting teachers
   - in classrooms, supporting students
   - meeting with teachers (no students) during specials and grade-level meetings
   - required responsibilities such as door duty and lunchroom duty
   - teaching students outside of the classroom (pullout)
   - planning for professional development, facilitation, and so forth
   - analyzing data and similar activities
   - administrative or clerical duties, such as entering data and organizing books
   - attending outside meetings, workshops, and so forth

REFLECTION, EVALUATION, AND PLANNING

1. How have you divided your day to move tasks you do alone, such as writing reports and entering data, to times when teachers and students are not available?

2. How much time do you spend working with teachers in ways that seem to make a difference, such as team meetings, one-on-one coaching cycles (see "The Coaching Cycle" on page 54), and study groups (see "Planning a Teachers' Study Group" on page 192)? If it is not enough, how do you plan to make time to do those things?

3. If you are struggling to make time for the most valuable coaching activities, how can you collaborate with the principal gain support (see "Communicating with the Principal" on page 177)? How can you make the case about where you need to focus your time? To garner support from the principal and teachers, can you supply documentation—for example, agendas from study groups and student achievement data from teachers you are coaching—indicating change that has resulted from you using your time optimally?

4. What articles can you share with administrators and teachers to help them understand your role? For example, which articles from the Literacy Coaches Clearinghouse (www.literacycoachingonline.org) support and advocate for the work of coaches?

Literacy Coach Activities Pie Chart

This graph represents a day ☐   Date_____

This graph represents a week ☐   Date_____

Example Literacy Coach Activities Pie Chart

This graph represents a day ☐   Date_____

This graph represents a week ☑   Date_10/15–19_____

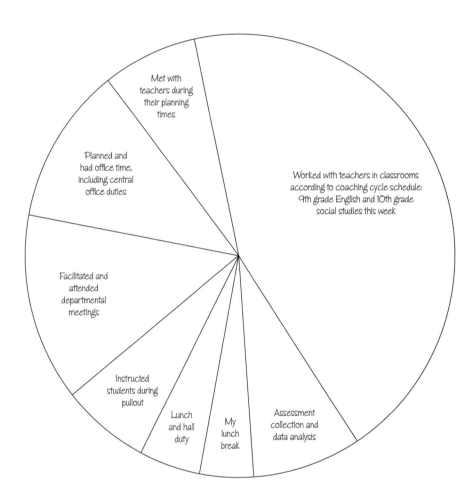

Met with teachers during their planning times

Planned and had office time, including central office duties

Worked with teachers in classrooms according to coaching cycle schedule: 9th grade English and 10th grade social studies this week

Facilitated and attended departmental meetings

Instructed students during pullout

Lunch and hall duty

My lunch break

Assessment collection and data analysis

Keeping a Transparent Schedule

TARGET

Elementary ✓   Middle School/High School ✓

Where is our literacy coach? This common question among teachers stems from the fact that, in many schools, literary coaching is a relatively new position. Both coaches and other school staff have to work to define and appreciate the position and to understand its potential to benefit teachers, students, and the infrastructure. The struggle to define coaching is what sometimes leads some teachers to wonder, when they are feeling overwhelmed with their goals and hopes for their students, What is the literacy coach doing when not in my room?

Another potential pitfall for coaches is the important partnerships they have with their principals. As administrators recognize coaches' expertise and support, they may begin to approach you more frequently for input and help. Principals may sometimes stop you in the hallway on your way to a scheduled classroom visit and to talk "for a minute." Although delaying your arranged time for classroom support may give the principal some needed assistance, it may hurt the relationship you have with the teacher whose visit was postponed.

You can overcome some of these difficulties by keeping your daily or weekly schedule posted in a public place, such as on the wall outside your office, in the teacher's lounge, or near the office mailboxes. These three guidelines may help you structure and adhere to your schedule:

- Avoid the temptation to give yourself more daily planning periods than a teacher has. This will build a positive, honest picture of the work you do.
- Have prepared responses for those who might unintentionally pull you from your schedule. For example, "Ms. Smith has arranged her morning to accommodate my visit." Or, "I have a planning period at 1:10. I'll come right to your office then." Or, "Mr. Jones and I worked for several hours to set up coteaching at this time. I think it would hurt our partnership if I didn't come on time."
- Remember that adhering to a schedule builds trust with teachers and principals and may contribute to building a productive learning community. This is a key role

for coaches because good learning communities have been positively correlated to student achievement (The Searle Funds at the Chicago Community Trust, 2007).

References for further learning

Allen, J. (2006). *Becoming a literacy leader: Supporting learning and change.* Portland, ME: Stenhouse.

The Searle Funds at the Chicago Community Trust. (2007). *A school's framework for improving literacy instruction: Seven dimensions of school practice.* Urbana-Champagne: University of Illinois.

GOALS

- To define the multifaceted role of the literacy coach in a school, especially if the position is new.
- To make the literacy coach's whereabouts known to all staff members.
- To help literacy coaches avoid being deterred from scheduled classroom appointments.
- To make the coach more realistic about what can be accomplished in any given week.
- To build trusting relationships.

IMPLEMENTATION

1. Using the Literacy Coaching Schedule, or modifying it to fit your needs, create a weekly schedule that clearly details your whereabouts and briefly notes the nature of your work.
2. Post the schedule on the outside of your door or in a place visible to all staff, such as the main office or the teacher's lounge.
3. Use a staff meeting or grade-level meetings (see "Organizing Grade-Level and Department Meetings" on page 188) to make a one-time explanation of your schedule, where it is posted, and how you will note changes over the week.
4. If you must make changes due to unanticipated events, such as a fire drill or sick day, annotate the schedule to show that you are committed to staying "transparent" throughout the week. This might include noting changes you had to make because a teacher was absent or you were called out of the building by the district office. Some coaches write weekly plans on a large, laminated, blank schedule and then mark changes as necessary.
5. Consider adding a second sheet that has a space for teachers to write notes to you, request a meeting, cancel an ill-timed visit, or ask to be included in your next schedule at a particular time.

REFLECTION, EVALUATION, AND PLANNING

1. What are the various places your schedule could be displayed? Which of those has best access for all staff?

2. How is the format and structure of your schedule working for you? Does it clearly show what is critical for your staff to see, such as the content of your work, details, and locations?

3. If you are including a sheet for staff to leave you notes, how are they using it?

4. How often was your schedule changed and what were the reasons? Were they acceptable to you? To your staff? How are you helping your principal and district acknowledge the importance of a coach adhering to a schedule and keeping appointments?

5. What method do you use to revise your schedule if it changes? Does it convey a message of transparency?

6. Does your schedule reflect the same amount of planning time as that of classroom teachers? If not, how can you revise is, knowing that appearing to have more planning time than teachers may affect your collegial relationships with them?

Literacy Coaching Schedule

	Monday	Tuesday	Wednesday	Thursday	Friday
8:30					
9:00					
9:30					
10:00					
10:30					
11:00					
11:30					
12:00					
12:30					
1:00					
1:30					
2:00					
2:30					
3:00					
3:30					
4:00					

Example Literacy Coaching Schedule

	Monday	Tuesday	Wednesday	Thursday	Friday
8:30	Staff Mtg. No lit. on agenda	7:45–8:45 Comprehension Book Club 8:45 Door Duty	4th Grade Team Meeting	2nd Grade Team Meeting	Attend District Coaches Meeting
9:00	Coaching Cycle Guided Reading Room 106	Observation Room 210		Coaching Cycle Mentor Text Room 211	
9:30	↓	↓	Coaching Cycle Guided Reading Room 106	↓	
10:00	Coteach Guided Reading	5th Grade Team Meeting	↓	Planning Period in Book Room	
10:30	Mentor New Teacher Room 311		Mentor New Teacher Room 311	Mentor New Teacher Room 111	↓
11:00	↓	Mentor New Teacher Room 111	↓	↓	
11:30	Lunch	↓	Lunch	Lunch	
12:00	Lunch Duty	Lunch Duty	Lunch Duty	Lunch Duty	Lunch
12:30	Coaching Cycle Mentor Texts Room 211	Lunch	Administer K Assessments in 108	6th Grade Team Meeting	Lunch Duty
1:00	Meet with Principal, re: week's schedule	Coaching Cycle Vocab. S.S. Room 306	Administer K Assessments in 107	School Literacy Team (released for current Align Project)	Coaching Cycle Vocab. S.S. Room 306
1:30	Planning Period in Lit Room	↓	Planning Period In Book Room	↓	↓
2:00	Coteaching Vocabulary Lesson Room 309	Planning Period in Lit Room	Meet with Parent Group		Meet with Principal, re: debriefing schedule
2:30	Enter Ass't Data	Enter Ass't Data			Planning Period in Book Room
2:45	Guided Reading Study Group	1st Grade Team Meeting	3rd Grade Team Meeting	Writing Study Group	Door Duty

Keeping a Coach's Log

TARGET

Elementary ✓   Middle School/High School ✓

Many districts are field-testing to determine and record the support literacy coaches provide to school staffs. They need to know what coaches will do, how effective their work will be, and how to best advocate to preserve the coach's position. To contribute to this effort, literacy coaches must find ways to document the local support they provide. Some coaches find it helpful to keep a log that records the actions they take on behalf of literacy.

Literacy coaches can also use logs to inform local principals about how they spend their time. With knowledge of what coaches are doing, principals can forge the kind of partnerships with their coaches that can maximize the benefits of their work. Coaches must rely on the support of their principals to be effective, and a log can be an important part of garnering that support. (See "Communicating with the Principal" on page 177.)

In addition, literacy coaches can use daily, weekly, or monthly logs themselves as starting points to reflect on how they are spending their time, what types of activities are most helpful, and how they might revise their schedules to be most productive.

The log does not have to be extremely detailed, unless you want to document those details. For most purposes, the basic categories of what you do are enough. For instance, this entry in a log would clearly present an image of one day's work:

Wednesday
- In classrooms, worked with two new teachers for an hour a piece.
- Helped new teacher organize an assessment notebook to store informal running records.
- Met with 5th grade study group after school—investigating vocabulary development.
- Facilitated two grade-level meetings: 5th grade during their specials and 1st grade before school.
- During planning researched resources for new study group on guided reading— begins in two weeks.

- In teacher-to-teacher classroom—coaching cycle for vocabulary (both from study group).
- No lunch or door duty today.
- One parent call about student.
- Brief meeting with principal.

GOALS

- To help document the literacy coach's job-related activities for the coach, for school administrators, and to fill any central office requests for such an account.
- To facilitate communication with others about literacy coaching activities.
- To maintain a record to communicate with staff.
- To provide information for the coach to reflect about activities.

IMPLEMENTATION

1. Decide on a log format that best suits your needs. You can use the following Coach's Log tool, or carry a small notebook that stays with you throughout the day. You may also rely on the weekly schedule posted on your door (see "Keeping a Transparent Schedule" on page 23).
2. Set up a routine to most efficiently enter the information from your notebook or schedule into digital form for storage and printing. You might carry over the information once a week or make entries at the end of each day.
3. Use an entry format that allows you to transfer the data quickly. For example, you might use bulleted statements instead of a narrative format.
4. At the end of a week, a month, the quarter, and the school year, review the log and critically analyze how you used your time. You may find it helpful to document your response to the day's or week's activities, but your responses may not be something you enter in the log.
5. Discuss the potential of sharing the log with your principal. Would the principal benefit from reviewing the log on a weekly, monthly, or quarterly basis? Many coaches report that submitting a weekly log stapled to the same week's schedule provides a strong foundation for the principal-coach partnership and discussions about how the coach supports staff in the school.

REFLECTION, EVALUATION, AND PLANNING

1. How do the activities listed in your log compare to your planned schedule?

2. Which activities are consuming the majority of your time? Which take up the least amount of time? How does that distribution match your and you school's vision for the role of a literacy coach? If how you spend your time doesn't align with the vision for the literacy coach's role, what can you change to reconcile the two?

3. Do you notice trends in your logs? Are there trends that suggest that you need to revise your schedule? Do the trends match up with your vision of an effective coach?

Coach's Log

Date _____

Date _____

Date _____

Date _____

Date _____

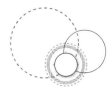

Analyzing the School's Literacy Culture

TARGET
Elementary ✓   Middle School/High School ✓

Taking the pulse of a school's literacy culture can bring to light school values and what might be going on in classrooms. If your school is fortunate enough to have both a coach and a school literacy team (see "Creating a School Literacy Team" on page 181), the trends revealed in the survey can inform how the school moves both teachers and students forward in literacy.

The following Assessing Literacy Culture survey asks teachers to rank how often—seldom, sometimes, or regularly—they follow literacy practices that the coach and school recommend. It not only acknowledges what they value, it documents it. You can customize the following list of questions or construct your own list. You can even adapt the survey for a particular grade level or group of grades.

The important thing is that your list reflects what is important to teachers and what is valued and required by their curriculum. For instance, you might exclude item 5, "Time is set aside for a volume of independent-level reading," if teachers and the curriculum do not acknowledge and honor the importance of having students practice what the they have been taught during the teacher's direct instruction on comprehension strategies, phonics, phonemic awareness, genres, and so forth. However, the items you exclude from the original survey can be telling and give you insights about what you should introduce to the staff in the future.

You can also use the items on the list as a set of goals, behaviors, and activities that the school is moving toward. The survey can create a language common to all teachers in a grade and across all grades in a school. Although the survey can only provide formative information once, it can become a pre- and post-assessment to see whether teachers report a change in their behaviors.

GOALS

- To establish a baseline of the school's or grade level's existing literacy culture.
- To collect formative data to make plans for professional development and change.

- To provide pre- and post-change data to evaluate the effectiveness of school or grade level's efforts to move their literacy culture forward.

IMPLEMENTATION

1. Meet with your school literacy team, grade-level representatives, or even all teachers during an all-school staff development meeting. Decide whether the items on this survey reflect what matters to them and what is required as part of their curriculum.
2. Come to consensus on a final list and distribute it at a meeting of all teachers.
3. Call for questions about the definitions of any of the items. Confirm that everyone is rating their implementation based on the same understanding.
4. You may not need to ask teachers to write names on the list, but they should make a copy of their own lists if you plan to use the survey as a pre- and post-assessment.
5. Collect copies of the surveys and compile the data into one summary sheet.
6. Begin to analyze the summary, mining it deeply for information such as:

   - trends
   - what is going well
   - surprises
   - what could be a quick win
   - what would require long-term work, even multiple years
   - what trends indicate a need for a professional development plan
   - what trends are a result of not having enough resources

7. Based on the data, make a preliminary action plan that includes professional development plans, short-term and long-term goals, and time lines. For example, if you discover that significantly less than half of the teachers noted that their students were conversing about books, you might do the following:

   - Share background about literature circles with teachers.
   - Help teachers plan for literature circles by preparing role cards and grouping students for instruction. Then help choose books for groups based on students' levels and interests.
   - Model the implementation of literature circles for the teachers.
   - Observe and provide feedback as the teachers gradually take over the responsibility of running the literature circles.
   - Meet regularly with teachers to plan and debrief.

8. Return to the group who first came to consensus on the items and share the outcomes of the survey. If you are working with only a representative group of teachers, you should still share the summary with the entire staff.

REFLECTION, EVALUATION, AND PLANNING

1. In what areas do these teacher self-reports not match your classroom and building observations? How will you approach that discrepancy?
2. Where do you need to revise the survey? Which items could you eliminate because they do not reflect your school's vision? Given that vision and teacher responses, which items should you add to the survey?
3. How do outcomes on items correlate to each other? Responses on like items should correspond. If they do not, how can you approach staff about these topics?
4. Based on the survey trends, which activities will best suit the action plan you are developing?

Assessing Literacy Culture

	Seldom	Sometimes	Regularly
1. Students enjoy reading.			
2. Teachers read aloud to students.			
3. Classroom libraries are appealing and well used.			
4. Classrooms use informational texts, magazines, and newspapers.			
5. Time is set aside for a volume of independent-level reading.			
6. Students know how to select a book at an appropriate level.			
7. Students have conversations with each other, not just answer teacher questions, about books they read.			
8. Students share their reading and writing orally through performance, such as Reader's Theatre.			
9. Students demonstrate confidence using comprehension strategies.			
10. Teachers regularly discuss with each other their instruction and professional reading.			
11. School librarians are valued resources to students and teachers.			
12. Students help each other become better readers across and within grade levels.			
13. Classrooms and hallways stimulate interest in literacy.			
14. Student writing reflects voice, authenticity, and purpose.			
15. Students write regularly for a variety of purposes.			

Planning a Professional Development Workshop

TARGET
Elementary ✓   Middle School/High School ✓

There are countless reasons to hold inservice training in schools. For instance, if a district adopts a new approach to reading comprehension, the coach may be asked to model the strategies teachers are expected to use. Or the literacy coach may want to provide teachers with professional development about comprehension strategies because students struggle with extended responses on their state reading test.

In most cases, the whole school needs to hear about certain concepts and be familiar with the language before coaches try to differentiate their support for grade level's and teachers' needs. For example, a coach may hold an inservice workshop for the whole staff about the importance of differentiating book levels for all students. After the basic overview to the whole group, the coach may begin working with primary teachers to move toward guided-reading groups and with middle school teachers to begin partner reading.

In any case, literacy coaches may know the content of the inservice training but wonder how to pull it together. Whatever the size, topic, or reason, you can use some or all of the items on Planning School-Based Inservice Training: My Checklist to help plan for and reflect on the outcomes of the professional development.

When you are planning the inservice training, remember that

- Whole-group inservice training is most useful to introduce or explain a topic. The real work with teachers will likely take place in the follow-ups to whole-group professional development sessions, such as during grade-level meetings (see "Organizing Grade-Level and Department Meetings" on page 188), in coaching cycles (see "The Coaching Cycle" on page 54), in study groups (see "Planning a Teachers' Study Group" on page 192), and in book clubs (see "Forming a Teacher Book Club" on page 196).
- The more carefully planned and prepared the training, the more confident you will feel. You will also be more ready to handle any surprises during inservice training.

- Inservice training in which you only lecture will not hold the attention of teachers or have the potential for action. Adult learning theory reminds us that, for every 10 minutes of listening, adults need 2 minutes of processing and reflection time.
- Variety in inservice training will hold the interest and support the topic better than a single form of presentation. Combinations of viewing and debriefing videos, reading, talking, and listening give teachers a chance to think about the topic in a range of ways.

GOALS

- To carefully think through all plans and goals for successful inservice training.
- To base inservice training on audience interaction and problem solving.
- To use audience response to the inservice training to enrich future presentations.

IMPLEMENTATION

1. To help structure your planning, familiarize yourself with Planning School-Based Inservice Training: My Checklist.
2. Use teacher surveys, informal observations, curriculum requirements, and test scores to identify topics for presentation.
3. Make a rough agenda for the inservice training, such as:

   8:00 Welcome/agenda/outcomes

   8:05 Activator

   8:20 Brief introduction to strategy of visualization

   8:30 Short article to be read individually

   8:40 Small-group discussion about the article

   8:55 Report out on key points from the article

   9:15 8-minute video of 2nd grade visualization activity

   9:25 Small-group discussion about the video

   9:35 Distribute handouts describing visualization protocol

        Sign up for coaching cycles or study groups on visualization

        Fill out and hand in inservice evaluations

4. Carefully compare your preliminary agenda to the checklist items. If items are missing from checklist, add them on the blank lines.
5. After the training, summarize the evaluations (see "Evaluating Literacy Professional Development Workshops" on page 46) and look for trends that can guide your future actions.

REFLECTION, EVALUATION, AND PLANNING

1. What items on the checklist contributed to your confidence before and during the inservice training? Were there items that were not supportive enough? How will you revise them to be more helpful in the future?

2. What challenges arose during the inservice training that the checklist didn't address? How will you revise the list before your next inservice training to help with that challenge in the future?

3. Did you plan follow-up coaching support after your whole-school professional development? What level of interest did teachers show for follow-up, as indicated by who signed up for a study group or coaching cycle?

Planning School-Based Inservice Training: My Checklist

Before planning, I have decided on:

☐ A focused topic based on research, standards, and a staff needs assessment.

☐ Which essential information is needed to understand my topic.

☐ Whether the size of my topic fits into my session time.

☐ What I want people to walk away knowing or being able to do.

☐ How teachers might best learn this topic.

☐ Which visuals to use (e.g., videos, PowerPoint presentations, pictures, or poster boards).

☐ How to make the topic look different if it is already familiar to my audience.

☐ Which classroom teachers might join me to copresent.

☐ Which samples of student (most important) and teacher work highlight my topic.

☐ The date to distribute first copy of my presentation agenda (1 week prior).

☐ The date to distribute second copy of my presentation agenda (1 day prior).

☐ _____

☐ _____

My plan includes:

☐ An activator to prepare my audience to receive and interact with the information.

☐ Direct, explicit information the audience needs to understand my content.

☐ Handouts that briefly highlight my topic's essential content.

☐ Handouts for implementing my topic (e.g., example lesson or graphic organizer).

☐ A balance between my presentation's format, variety, and audience interaction.

☐ Forms of audience participation that allow me to check for understanding.

☐ A format and audience interaction plan appropriate to my topic and the room size.

☐ Frequent stopping points for audience to practice or discuss new information.

☐ A plan for audience questions, specifying if they are allowed during or only after the presentation and if they should be verbal or written.

☐ Pictures or videos of students to engage my audience.

☐ A plan for resistant participants (e.g., don't focus on "unhappy" faces).

☐ An evaluation form copied and ready for distribution.

☐ _____

☐ _____

If I use visuals:

☐ My videos are brief and carefully edited.

☐ My videos are going to be shown in short segments, offering many opportunities for conversation.

☐ My PowerPoint slides have limited amounts of print with the largest font possible.

☐ My PowerPoint slides are just bulleted highlights—not a copy of everything I say.

☐ Poster boards are large enough for all participants to see.

☐ Handouts are clean, focused, dated, and include the credit name and organization.

☐ _____

☐ _____

After rehearsing, I know:

☐ My presentation fits into the time frame and is appropriately paced.

☐ The topic does not feel too big.

☐ My information is explicit.

☐ Teachers are likely to say "I could go back to my classroom and try this."

☐ There is a balance of presentation of content and processing time.

☐ _____

On the day of my inservice training, I come early to:

☐ Touch base with a conference coordinator or facilitator when possible.

☐ Check out the location and layout of my room.

☐ Rearrange chairs and tables if needed and if possible.

☐ Try out equipment (e.g., DVD or LCD projector).

☐ _____

☐ _____

After my inservice, I ask myself:

☐ Did I feel as though I accomplished my goal?

☐ Is there evidence that my inservice topic or strategy is being implemented?

☐ Have evaluations been summarized, tallied, and mined for information?

☐ Did presentation evaluations suggest changes in future presentations?

☐ If appropriate, did I clearly list the possibility of voluntary follow-up to this presentation, such as working with grade-level groups, study groups, or coaching cycles?

☐ _____

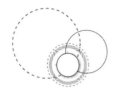

Using People Search as a Meeting Icebreaker

TARGET

Elementary ✓   Middle School/High School ✓

Sometimes the members of an audience haven't worked or interacted with each other before, such as when the coach is presenting at a conference, working in a new location, or has had many staff additions at a school. Or the members of a group may know each other well but be under stress or feel overwhelmed with the amount of information being passed on to them. One helpful tool to relax or thaw a crowd is an icebreaker to give people an opportunity to talk to each other.

A particularly effective icebreaker for literacy groups is People Search, which involves books and memories of books. Each person receives a form to complete and, for each cell, needs to search out a person in the room who fits the description. For instance, one cell says, "Find someone who has saved a book from childhood." Another asks for a person who writes poetry.

In addition to encouraging people to start talking before you present, the icebreaker begins a routine that effective presenters tend to follow: allow people to move around and, more important, to talk to each other for brief periods throughout the presentation, workshop, or inservice training. On evaluation surveys, one of the most common responses to this type of format is, "Thanks for letting us talk to each other about the topics you presented."

After allowing time for participants to talk to each other and fill in the form, the coach calls everyone back together and begins to review the form, asking questions like, Did you find anyone who writes poetry?, When that person is acknowledged, the coach can also follow up with questions like, What kind of poetry?, or, Do you enjoy presenting poetry to your students? Do you ever read your poetry to them?

Icebreakers like this may take 20 minutes to introduce, fill out, and process, but it is usually worth the time. Icebreakers relax people; set a tone; and, in subtle but important ways, let the coach become familiar with some of the audience members' interests. Later on, you can use this knowledge as the basis for brief one-on-one talks that help you build a stronger working relationship. You can also build on this information during the remainder of the workshop.

GOALS

- To prompt informal literacy discussions before beginning a literacy-based professional development session or group meeting.
- To provide the literacy coach with anecdotal information about how individuals in the group feel about reading, writing, and literature.
- To start people talking to each other to promote discussion later when the coach gives the audience a chance to process what they have heard.

IMPLEMENTATION

1. Select an icebreaker that fits the size of your room. Consider whether participants have enough room to walk around and interact.
2. Adapt the activity to fit the topic of your presentation. For instance, if it focuses on writing, add more cells that deal directly with writing.
3. Make copies for everyone in the group. If extra people show up, form pairs.
4. When the session begins, briefly welcome everyone, distribute the form, and give directions. Start the ball rolling by telling people which cell they can put your name in. For instance, "Put my name in '. . . writes poetry' because I do!"
5. Give people about 5–10 minutes to move around, talk, and fill out the form.
6. Circulate around the room, listening to conversations but not filling out a form yourself. Be alert for interesting facts to use when processing the whole-group discussion.
7. Note if someone is hesitant to move about the room. Chat with them to see if they can put your name in any other cell or steer them toward someone.
8. When forms are finished or the allotted time has passed, ask people to return to their seats. Some coaches present a prize, such as a children's book or writing pad, to the person who finishes the grid first. The prize should match the theme of the presentation.
9. For each of the cells, call on people to share the name of someone they wrote down. Work briefly through several or all of the cells, depending on time. Ask people to elaborate when it will be interesting to the group.

REFLECTION, EVALUATION, AND PLANNING

1. How did the group respond to the activity? Were they interacting as you had hoped?

2. Which cells on the icebreaker sheet inspired the best conversations between teachers? Were there some cells you should eliminate in the future? If so, what other topics can you use to replace them?

3. How would you characterize your processing of the whole-group discussion at the end? Were you able to rely on the comments from the group to carry the discussion?

4. What information, if any, did the processing provide that helped you know how to partner people later in the presentation or meeting?

5. Which information from the icebreaker were you able to use at subsequent points in the meeting? If it was too much information to remember, is there a way you can quietly jot down a few notes as people are sharing or after the sharing is complete?

People Search: Finding Writers and Readers

Find someone who . . .

is currently reading or has recently read something that is on the best-sellers list	has saved a book from childhood	keeps a diary or journal	has been part of a writing group
has sponsored a writing group in school	has had something published	has a favorite kind of pen	writes poetry
is in a book club	writes or regularly reads a blog	has more than one library card	has written a letter to the editor
has an autographed book	writes with his/her left hand	is a great speller	sends and receives text messages

People Search: Finding Writers and Readers

Find someone who . . .

Evaluating Literacy Professional Development Workshops

TARGET

Elementary ✓   Middle School/High School ✓

When a literacy coach works one-on-one, there is direct, on-the-spot feedback. But literacy coaches also work with their staffs in larger settings, such as small groups in grade-level teams or book clubs (see "Forming a Teacher Book Club" on page 196) and large groups that can include all staff members. How do you collect feedback—the kind of feedback that helps you determine your next steps—from larger groups?

Large-group inservice training (see "Planning a Professional Development Workshop" on page 36) can include teachers with significantly different needs, so it is particularly important to hear feedback from more than a few participants. With the whole-group inservice training as the foundation of common knowledge, the responses can guide your smaller group, follow-up sessions.

One way to get this feedback is to distribute a form that participants fill out at the end of the inservice training. In many situations, teachers may feel more comfortable if their responses are anonymous. However, it is usually helpful to ask informants to include their grade level or area of responsibility so that you can use that information to identify trends. After the literacy coach establishes relationships with the teachers that are built on trust, anonymity may not be as important.

Once teachers know that the coach is dedicated to supporting them—not evaluating them as teachers or speaking about their challenges to anyone, including the principal—then teachers will begin to use the form to address the content without a personal edge. It takes time to build this kind of trusting response.

Coaches have reported that using the same format on their professional development evaluations helps teachers become familiar with how to express their feelings about the inservice training.

GOALS

- To evaluate staff response to a literacy coach's professional development session.
- To evaluate staff response to a consultant or presenter or workshop attended by staff.
- To evaluate the future needs of the staff.
- To help plan subsequent professional development sessions, workshops, or registrations to workshops outside of the school.
- To assess where a particular professional development session will fit into the overall plan for the school's literacy support.

IMPLEMENTATION

1. On the Professional Development Evaluation template, fill in the date, purpose/content/topic(s) of session, and presenter(s) before making copies to distribute.
2. On the meeting agenda, include "inservice training evaluation" or "inservice training feedback" as the final item, allowing 5–10 minutes for participants to fill out the survey. Be careful not to keep staff past the posted ending time.
3. If the evaluation is anonymous, identify a container for the teachers to deposit the evaluation forms. Avoid having teachers hand completed forms to someone, because it may suggest that responses are not anonymous.
4. Summarize the survey information. Note that quantitative scores are tabulated and anecdotal comments are recorded.
5. Analyze the compiled feedback to improve future professional development sessions.
   - **Participants:** Determine if there are differences in the responses from teachers and support staff. If so, how can you make the sessions more informative to the different populations on the staff? Is it a good idea to include the entire staff in this type of professional development?
   - **Likert Scale Ratings:** Identify which areas had the highest and lowest ratings. For those areas scoring 3s and 4s, examine the successful components of the professional development session. How can you capture those components and apply them to future sessions? For those areas scoring 1s and 2s, think about what went wrong. How can you improve them in future sessions?
   - **Open Responses:** This part of the evaluation form takes more time, thought, and effort from the participants. They usually only write open responses if something has made a profoundly positive or negative impression on them. Any comments repeated on multiple evaluations deserve your time and attention. Make sure you address the issue in future sessions.

6. If response is not positive, visit small groups of teachers, such as grade-level or content-area teams, to brainstorm what will meet their needs.

REFLECTION, EVALUATION, AND PLANNING

1. How did the teacher feedback match your own observation of the session?

2. Which information on the form suggests that you did or didn't meet the goals of your session?

3. What trends indicate how to differentiate future professional development sessions? For example, does the survey suggest that kindergarten teachers found a guided-reading service inappropriate?

4. What environmental elements, such as seating, sound, and room size, were obstacles to teacher engagement? How can you change the setting for future inservice sessions? For instance, which neighboring institutions, such as banks or libraries, can you use without charge? If there are none, can they still be used sometimes for variety and to show that you respect teacher responses to the environment?

5. What key teacher suggestions will you incorporate into future sessions?

6. Brainstorm with staff about ways to determine whether the content you are presenting is making a difference with student learning and teacher instruction.

Professional Development Evaluation

Date:

Purpose/Content/Topic(s) of Session:

Presenter(s):

Grade Level or School Position (e.g., Administration or LDR) _____

	Not at All ⟶ Strongly Agree			
	1	2	3	4
1. This activity increased my literacy knowledge and skills.				
2. The relevance of this activity to the instruction in my classroom (or school responsibility) was clear.				
3. The material was presented in an organized, easily understandable manner.				

4. What was the best feature of this session?

5. What might improve future sessions of this type?

6. What follow-up support, such as grade-level discussions, study groups, or modeling, might be necessary to continue your learning about the topic discussed today?

7. Other comments I wish to offer:

How to Get Invited into Classrooms

TARGET
Elementary ✓   Middle School/High School ✓

Coaches frequently ask, "How do I get teachers to invite me into their classrooms?" No one asks that question more frequently than a coach who is new to a school or new to a coaching position.

One inventive coach new to a school in a large urban district, Evelyn Acevedo-Nolfi, developed a form she called a *literacy menu*. She designed and printed the form herself and then, with her principal's support, put a copy in each teacher's mailbox. Above the columns for classroom environment additions and demonstration lessons, she included a short introduction: "This is a list of items that I can do in your classrooms to help you. Please check any of the items below and place this form in my mailbox. I will come in to assist you as soon as I become available."

Not only had Ms. Acevedo-Nolfi offered to help teachers, she had subtlety accomplished several other important things. First, she made it clear that she would wait for an invitation to visit a classroom. This may have comforted some teachers nervous about her new role. The items on her list were also a strong message about what she considered important. Finally, it acknowledged that she was ready to help where needed, which conveyed that she recognizes classroom teachers' important work.

Within six months of distributing the list, Ms. Acevedo-Nolfi had not only gained entrance into classrooms, but she had also moved beyond the list and was involved in multiple coaching cycles (see "The Coaching Cycle" on page 54) with teachers trying new strategies and techniques themselves.

One of the reasons for Ms. Acevedo-Nolfi's success was her interest, from the beginning, in forming a learning community. Each time she entered a classroom, she looked for appropriate opportunities to move teacher-literacy coach partnerships forward. She used her menu as a step toward that end.

You have to find your own way to deliver a message of willingness to work and learn with teachers, but the following Literacy Menu is certainly a strong option. Keep in mind that the menu is only one element of the continuing effort to build relationships and interact with teachers.

GOALS

- To gain respectful entrance to teachers' classrooms.
- To show respect for teacher choice.
- To build relationships of trust with teachers.
- To send subtle messages about the kinds of literacy strategies and curriculum considered best practice for reading and writing.

IMPLEMENTATION

1. Become familiar with the materials and resources available to teachers (see "Analyzing Primary Classroom Resources" on page 200 and "Analyzing Classroom Libraries" on page 204), and compile a list of coaching services that could fill gaps.
2. Construct a list of services that fall under the category of best practice.
3. Using the Literacy Menu tool, or by developing your own form, put together a list of the services you are willing to offer. Show it to the principal to ensure that you have administrative support.
4. Distribute the menu in the staff's mailboxes or present copies at a staff meeting.
5. Include a due date on the form. If teachers ask for more than one type of help, either decide yourself or ask the teacher to prioritize them.
6. After you've collected and prioritized the forms, begin to construct a schedule (see "Keeping a Transparent Schedule" on page 23). Try to meet informally with each teacher to set up times and dates.
7. When you've completed the schedule, first share it with the principal to make sure that you have support for your plan to allocate services. Set aside a time for a weekly meeting to keep your principal up-to-date on your schedule, but make it clear that you will not be reporting what you see in classrooms (see "Communicating with the Principal" on page 177).
8. Post the schedule on the outside of your door. Also send a copy to each of the teachers listed on the schedule, highlighting their particular time.

9. Commit to follow through with your schedule, unless it is out of your control. This commitment is as important as the service you provide because it shows teachers you are dependable and builds trust.

10. Remain dedicated to not report to anyone, including the principal, what you see in the classrooms that you visit. If even one teacher thinks that you reported your observations, it will hurt all relationships.

REFLECTION, EVALUATION, AND PLANNING

1. What are the trends among teachers who filled out and returned the menu?

2. How are you managing scheduling? Have you built in time lines so that teachers know that support in one area is only temporary until they can take responsibility themselves? Experiment with using some form of coaching contract (see "Coaching by Contract" on page 58) to define your time lines and roles.

3. Based on the responses, what do you need to revise on your menu? Which important forms of support are not on the list? Do you see the menu as a one-time introduction to acquaint the school with your services?

4. If you have already made visits, what items on the list best led to more substantive coaching interactions? For instance, helping to set up a classroom library can lead to deeper interest in fluency, independent reading, and motivation.

Literacy Menu

From the desk of _____

Date _____

This is a list of items that I can help you set up in your classrooms. Please check any of the items below and place this form in my mailbox. I will come in to assist you as soon as I become available.

Classroom Environment	Demonstration Lessons
☐ Organize classroom library	☐ Guided reading
☐ Level books for guided reading	☐ Read-Alouds/Think-Alouds
☐ Assess students	☐ Writer's Workshop
☐ Organize Writer's Workshop folders	☐ Shared/Interactive Writing*
☐ Set up a poetry corner	☐ DR-TA/DL-TA
☐ Locate and print poems	☐ Word Sorting
☐ Locate Reader's Theatre scripts	☐ Shared Reading*
☐ Set up a word wall	☐ WRAP/LEA*
	☐ Poem of the Week

☐ Other: _____

☐ Other: _____

* for K–1 classrooms

Teacher's Name _____ Room _____

Source: Adapted with permission from the work of Evelyn Acevedo-Nolfi, literacy coach at Avondale School, Chicago, Ill., and Wanda Williams-Sims, literacy coach at Jordan School, Chicago, Ill., 2007.

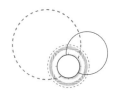

The Coaching Cycle

TARGET
Elementary ✓   Middle School/High School ✓

Coaching cycle is a term coined by national education consultant Diane Sweeney to describe her plan, or structure, for working one-on-one with teachers. Most acknowledge literacy coaches' powerful work in the small-group settings of grade-level meetings (see "Organizing Grade-Level and Department Meetings" on page 188), study groups (see "Planning a Teachers' Study Group" on page 192), and book clubs (see "Forming a Teacher Book Club" on page 196). Yet, working one-on-one with teachers remains a critical component of literacy coaching support in schools.

A coaching cycle is an efficient way to support individual teachers in a school within a structured framework that emphasizes students' learning goals. Working together one-on-one, a classroom teacher and a literacy coach collaborate to set student learning goals, construct an action plan, define responsibilities, set a time line, and identify ways to document whether their goals were reached.

There is nothing hit-or-miss about a coaching cycle. It generally lasts from six to nine weeks and requires an in-depth partnership between a teacher or pair of teachers and a coach. One important feature is that the teacher chooses the focus of the cycle. For some teachers, the coaching cycle may be as specific as the minilessons that introduce a writer's workshop. For others, it may be the complex and multifaceted practice of teaching small-group reading in the primary grades. Regardless of the focus, it should be rooted in the teacher and coach's combined examination of student data that supports the need for a coaching cycle.

Coaching cycles include regular planning sessions, which can be from 30 to 45 minutes once a week, and classroom visits while the teacher is instructing on the cycle activities, which can be from one to three times per week. Before beginning the cycle, you should create a contract (see "Coaching by Contract" on page 58) that carefully documents the coach's and teacher's responsibilities in the classroom and a time line for support.

Whole-school or multigrade workshops often precede one-on-one training, and these presentation topics might lend themselves to a coaching cycle. (See "Planning a Professional Development Workshop" on page 36 for more direction about these workshops.) For instance, in the case of the primary teachers, you might meet with all K–3 teachers and overview guided reading. In closing, you could offer to do two or three coaching cycles with people interested in learning more and who are willing to share their learning with other staff. In this way, all staff are aware of the language and the message, and teachers can decide when to begin and how it will affect their classrooms, fostering engagement at a deeper level than when change is mandated.

To help teachers organize their thoughts and aims for a coaching cycle, ask them to complete the Coaching Cycle Initiation form. From their responses, you should be able to glean their learning goals for students, which are the foundation for the coaching cycle. After the cycle, you can evaluate its effectiveness with the Coaching Cycle Evaluation form (see "Evaluating a Completed Coaching Cycle" on page 62).

GOALS

- To provide a tool for structuring the teacher's initiation of a coaching cycle.
- To give the literacy coach additional information about the teacher's understanding of how to choose a learning goal.

IMPLEMENTATION

1. Make it known that you are willing to work with teachers individually or in pairs to support a need they have established for their classrooms (see "How to Get Invited into Classrooms" on page 50).
2. Consider establishing some possible focuses by presenting multiple grade or content-based inservice workshops on topics relevant to the school's curriculum or that school scores indicate need improvement.
3. With the principal's support, give a presentation to the school to explain what a coaching cycle is and how it might look. It is helpful to show an example of a coaching cycle to help them visualize the partnership. The example should include a focus, a specific learning goal for students, the roles the coach and teacher will take, and a time line that includes when the teacher and coach will meet to discuss the cycle.
4. When a teacher requests a cycle, ask them to first complete the Coaching Cycle Initiation form.

REFLECTION, EVALUATION, AND PLANNING

1. Which information on the form provided the most important information needed to start a coaching cycle?

2. Beginning a coaching cycle requires agreement on roles and time lines. This can take the form of a coaching contract negotiated between the teacher and the coach (see "Coaching by Contract" on page 58). What items on the form are most helpful to construct that kind of coaching contract? Are there missing items that can present a challenge to negotiating a contract? Could you add questions to the form to avoid those problems?

3. A coaching cycle isn't always the best way to initially support teachers. If beginning with a coaching cycle did not work well with a particular teacher, how will you determine which other options—such as a book club (see "Forming a Teacher Book Club" on page 196), study group (see "Planning a Teachers' Study Group" on page 192), or initial work through grade-level team meetings (see "Organizing Grade-Level and Department Meetings" on page 188)—to explore first with other teachers?

Coaching Cycle Initiation

Name _____ Date _____
Grade Level/Content Area _____

Describe the instructional need you are seeing:

Do you have data that shows this need exists?

What have you already tried to do?

What materials have you been using?

What student learning outcomes would you like to see as a result of the cycle?

How might you assess progress?

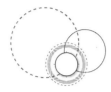

Coaching by Contract

TARGET
Elementary ✓   Middle School/High School ✓

Ideally, every time a teacher asks a coach for help, they enter into a goal-centered agreement before beginning one-on-one coaching, also known as a coaching cycle (see "The Coaching Cycle" on page 54). The teacher's goal is usually straightforward: to gain new knowledge, learn new instructional techniques, or problem solve about an existing classroom issue. The coach's role is more complex.

First, you want to fulfill the teacher's specific request for help, but you also want to lay the groundwork for the teacher to continue to grow and learn independently after the cycle is over. In addition, while you are working with one teacher, others may also be asking for support. Caring, committed literacy coaches are famous for taking on too much, leaving the coaches feeling burnt out and teachers feeling underserved.

Entering into a formalized agreement—an actual written contract—can make it easier for the coach to provide the necessary support, to build independence, and to balance commitments with other teachers. Finally, without a specific plan, coaching cycles can go astray even if you have the best of intentions.

Using the following Coaching Contract form, the coach and teacher collaborate and agree on and carefully note the answers to the following questions:

- What is the teacher's learning goal for the students? Answering this question keeps the focus on students and learning instead of on instruction or strategies.
- Is there documentation or evidence of the need for change? For example, has the teacher collected written literature responses that suggest comprehension problems, documented consistently low spelling scores, or analyzed test data that confirm problems with vocabulary development?
- Given the learning goal, what specific forms of coaching support—such as modeling, feedback, identification of new resources, or study through readings—will the teacher need?
- When will the coaching support begin and end?

- When will the teacher and coach meet to monitor progress toward achieving the students' learning goal?
- Will the teacher be willing to share the desired changes in student outcomes with other teachers?

Working one-on-one with teachers is an important part of the coach's job. Careful, written documentation can help structure a coaching workload that allows for both coaching cycles and the support for groups such as grade-level meetings (see "Organizing Grade-Level and Department Meetings" on page 188), school literacy teams (see "Creating a School Literacy Team" on page 181), and study groups (see "Planning a Teachers' Study Group" on page 192).

References for further learning

Spark+Innovation: http://www.sparkinnovate.com/pubs.html

Sweeney, D. (2007). Mirror, mirror, in the lab—process shows coaches clear reflections of their own practices. *Journal of Staff Development, 28*(1), 38–41.

GOALS

- To achieve a student learning goal identified by the teacher.
- To document the goal and roles of both the teacher and the coach.

IMPLEMENTATION

1. Solicit, encourage, or respond to a teacher's request for a coaching cycle.
2. Schedule a time with the teacher to fill out the Coaching Contract.
3. Work with the teacher to identify the students' learning problem, prompting the teacher for specifics that help clarify the source of the issue.
4. Establish a learning goal that could alleviate the problem. For instance, if a teacher notices that students do not demonstrate the ability to infer in a written response after reading, a student learning goal might be: "In a written response to reading, students will demonstrate at least one inference that either combines two pieces of information from the text to infer or combines a piece of information from the text with their own background knowledge."
5. Examine existing baseline documentation that the students are not currently exhibiting the goal.

6. Note how you will support the teacher—such as through modeling, forming a study group, watching a video, or providing feedback—to reach the learning goal for students.

7. Agree on time lines for both the length of the coaching cycle and how often you will meet.

8. Establish whether the teacher needs additional resources. For example, a coaching cycle to support small-group guided reading cannot proceed unless the teacher has enough instructional-level reading materials for the lessons.

9. Determine how and when you will measure progress during the coaching cycle and what students will have to demonstrate at the end of the cycle to suggest that they have reached the learning goal.

10. After the cycle, schedule a meeting to reflect on the components of the contract and what aspects you could adjust for future cycles.

REFLECTION, EVALUATION, AND PLANNING

1. Did you achieve the learning goal? If not, was it realistic? How could you have adjusted it?

2. Were the planning sessions adequate to understand each participant's role? Did you need more or less time?

3. Were the forms of coaching support appropriate to the learning goal? For example, did the teacher need more modeling? Did you need to observe more or provide more feedback on the teacher's implementation? Did the teacher need to read or study more to better understand the changes?

4. Is the teacher willing to share the cycle's lessons and outcomes with other teachers? If so, would it be most effective to share that information at a grade-level (see "Organizing Grade-Level and Department Meetings" on page 188) or all-school meeting?

Coaching Contract

Teacher _____ Coach _____

Dates of Coaching Cycle: From _____ to _____

Student Learning Goal:

Student data supporting need for student learning goal:	Meeting dates and times (to plan, debrief, monitor, etc.):
Instructional practices to learn, refine, and continue after cycle is completed:	Coaching strategies needed (modeling, observation, discussion, study group, etc.):
Coach responsibilities:	Teacher responsibilities:
Gradual release of responsibility from coach to teacher:	Documentation that student learning goal is achieved:
Date for end-of-cycle reflection meeting:	Possible opportunities to share student learning with other teachers:

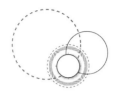

Evaluating a Completed Coaching Cycle

TARGET
Elementary ✓   Middle School/High School ✓

Once the coaching cycle is complete (see "The Coaching Cycle" on page 54), a thought-ful coach will evaluate its effectiveness by asking: Did the teacher feel supported? Did the coach feel effective? Was the learning goal realistic? You can take away much from both your reflections and those of the classroom teacher.

Each coach-teacher pairing has the potential to teach you something about coaching cycles and working with teachers, and reflecting at the end of each cycle can help you apply those lessons in your subsequent cycles. A completed Coaching Cycle Evaluation Form is the basis for this process.

At the end of the cycle, fill out an evaluation form, and then ask the teacher to complete one as well. Meet with the teacher to discuss your responses. Focus your discussion not on the content of the cycle, but on the process, time lines, roles and responsibilities of the coach and teacher, and whether it clearly centered on student learning. Closely compare the teacher's perspective to your own.

If the coaching cycle was successful, your evaluation discussion will support future coach-ing cycles with other teachers. However, a coaching cycle that didn't go as well as you expected may be just as valuable because you can learn from its pitfalls.

Effective literacy coaches work hard to build relationships and trust with teachers, and as a result, teachers should feel comfortable giving honest feedback. After you have com-pleted several cycles, go back and review the evaluation forms to identify trends. You can then use this information to guide your own professional development.

GOALS

• To give literacy coaches and teachers an opportunity to collect their thoughts, feelings, and responses to recently completed coaching cycles.

- To maintain records of teachers' and coaches' responses to coaching cycles.
- To use information from completed evaluation forms to improve future coaching cycles.
- To reflect on whether the roles, responsibilities, time lines, learning goals, and documentation fulfilled the teacher's and the coach's vision for the coaching cycle.
- To establish the coach as a colearner in the process of coaching cycles.

IMPLEMENTATION

1. Complete the form immediately after the coaching cycle.
2. One to two weeks after the coaching cycle, give this form to the teacher. Some coaches like to include a small token, such as a coffee coupon or chocolate bar, as a thank-you for completing the form.
3. Compare the teacher's responses to your own.
4. Meet with the teacher to briefly discuss the form and to clarify or discuss any of the responses, using prompts such as, "Tell me more about this."
5. Make notes about changes you will make the next time you do this coaching cycle.
6. Retain the form in a binder for reference.

REFLECTION, EVALUATION, AND PLANNING

1. How did the teacher respond to completing and submitting the form? If there was resistance, how can you support teachers' participation in the future?
2. What are the similarities and differences in teacher's views and your own about the coaching cycle?
3. Based on the information in this evaluation form, what changes can you make to future coaching cycles?
4. Was the post-coaching evaluation discussion productive? If not, what seemed to go wrong and where will you make changes? Was it possible that you had not established a trusting relationship during the coaching cycle? If so, what was the obstacle? What can you do to overcome it?
5. Based on completing this cycle, what further reading on the topic of coaching cycles or coaching in general do you need?
6. If this coaching cycle is not appropriate for all grade levels and content areas, how can you adapt it for others?

Coaching Cycle Evaluation Form

Teacher/Coach _____ Dates of Cycle _____

Grade Level _____ Subject Area/Focus of Cycle _____

	Not at All ⟶ Strongly Agree				
	1	2	3	4	5
1. The precycle planning prepared me for the cycle.					
2. The time lines for the cycle were appropriate.					
3. The roles and responsibilities for coach and teacher were clear and reasonable.					
4. This coaching cycle increased my knowledge in this area of instruction.					
5. There were sufficient materials to implement the coaching cycle.					
6. The next time I use this instructional process, I will implement strategies and activities that I learned in this coaching cycle.					
7. I am willing to share what I've learned with others.					

8. What was the best feature of this coaching cycle?

9. What would have improved the coaching cycle?

10. What else do you need from the literacy coach to feel confident in implementing what you've learned in this coaching cycle?

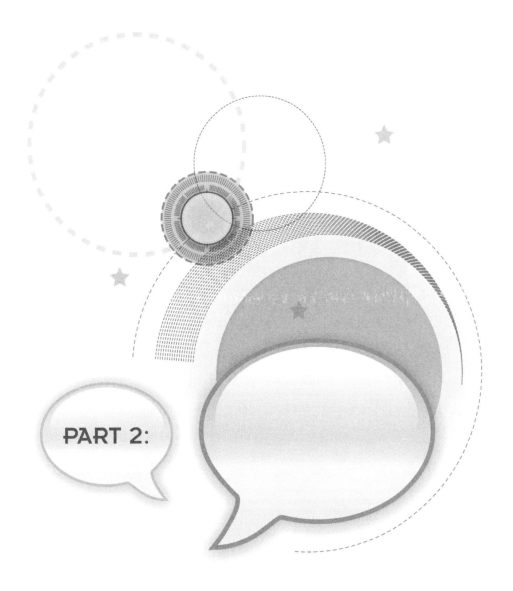

PART 2:

Professional Development

Teacher Instructional Knowledge Self-Rating

TARGET

Elementary ✓   Middle School/High School ✓

How would the teachers in your school answer this question: Given our curriculum and the materials we use, what instructional strategy knowledge do you need? This question can initiate a discussion that you, as a literacy coach, can moderate and enrich.

Sometimes teachers in the same grade level use strategies that appear to be at odds with each other. One of the first steps toward consistency within and across grade levels is to bring teachers together to identify strategies that everyone should be familiar with. The literacy coach can moderate this discussion by prompting where necessary and keeping the conversation focused on the school's vision or curriculum map, all while showing respect for what teachers see as important. The gathering is also a time for the coach to confirm which strategies are clearly acknowledged as best practices. You may even add some promising new strategies with which teachers are not yet familiar.

Once the group has agreed on a list, the coach can fill out the Instructional Strategy Knowledge Rating grid and distribute it at a subsequent meeting or to individual mailboxes. It's possible that some strategies—such as DR-TA (see "Introducing the DR-TA and DL-TA Strategies" on page 158) or KWL—would work for all grade levels, but some strategies—such as Shared Reading (see "Planning for Shared Reading" on page 132)—are only applicable to certain grade levels or content areas. Encourage teachers to include those strategies that have a proven track record for making a difference with students' literacy growth.

Depending on the school's culture, you can either ask teachers to return the forms with their names on them or anonymously. To preserve your relationships of trust with teachers, it may be safer to let the form be anonymous if the principal is heavily involved. If teachers turn in copies with their names, the literacy coach can begin grouping teachers who might form a study group about a particular topic (see "Planning a Teachers' Study Group" on page 192). Or the coach may schedule professional development sessions for those teachers. If teachers fill out the grids anonymously, the coach can identify areas of need and offer voluntary professional development to people interested in learning more about a certain topic.

Whether they fill out the grid with or without their names, the school staff becomes aware of strategies linked tightly to their curriculum, and you can gain a sense of where to focus support.

GOALS

- To begin creating a language and format for talking about a set of practices that reflect the common curriculum vision of all teachers in the school or of a group of grade levels or content areas.
- To identify a set of strategies essential to the school's established curriculum.
- To help teachers reflect on practices and strategies with which they feel secure and those with which they need additional support.

IMPLEMENTATION

1. Given your knowledge of the building and the support of the principal, either group teachers at grade-level meetings (see "Organizing Grade-Level and Department Meetings" on page 188) or at all-school staff meetings to begin the process of developing a list of strategies that support the school's curriculum. Enlist the voices of teachers as much as possible.
2. Prepare a copy of the grid based on the conclusions of the group meeting.
3. Distribute the Instructional Strategy Knowledge Rating grid and ask teachers to fill it out and return it to you. If you believe teachers may prefer anonymity, you may ask teachers to fill out the grid in their classrooms and put it in your mailbox. Ask teachers to make a copy for themselves before returning it to you.
4. Analyze the results to look for trends, and share trends with teachers and your principal at the next meeting. You may consider asking teachers to fill out the grid during a group meeting and to share their responses with others to immediately identify trends in their grade levels or content areas.
5. Plan to offer inservice training (see "Planning a Professional Development Workshop" on page 36) where the trends suggest a need, taking care to differentiate for those teachers who feel solid with the strategy. Asking for volunteers may not result in the teachers with the most need receiving assistance; however, requiring teachers to attend may not bring about the desired change. Wherever possible, consider study groups.
6. Do not attempt to do too much at once. Small steps can produce big changes.

REFLECTION, EVALUATION, AND PLANNING

1. How did teachers respond to the discussion about strategies? If they were not engaged, how can you change the conversation?

2. When you analyze the responses, either prioritize the trends by yourself or work with a small group of teachers for guidance on how to proceed with the list of strategy needs. Involving even only a few teachers can make your priority plan more credible with other teachers.

3. When sharing the results with teachers, consider using a poster or PowerPoint presentation to show the distribution of responses on the forms. You could also make paper copies of the survey summary and allow teachers to analyze and make plans by grade level.

4. How would you characterize the principal's role in the process? How did you take into account the principal's response to the summary?

PART 2

Instructional Strategy Knowledge Rating

Name _____ Grade _____ Date _____

Instructional Strategy	Never Heard of It	Heard of It	Tried It	Use It Regularly	Could Teach It
1.					
2.					
3.					
4.					
5.					
6.					
7.					
8.					
9.					
10.					
11.					
12.					
13.					

Teacher Comprehension Strategy Self-Rating

TARGET
Elementary ✓   Middle School/High School ✓

It is easy for schools to get caught up in phonics and word-study problems, and the public, out of frustration, frequently turns to them as a cause of reading problems. One of a literacy coach's most important jobs is to help the staff maintain a balanced approach to instruction. This requires a commitment to helping students increase their ability to comprehend both fiction and informational text. Addressing comprehension instruction requires a three-prong approach.

First, the coach must be an informal, nonevaluative presence in and out of classrooms, coteaching and offering coaching cycles (see "The Coaching Cycle" on page 54) and other support. The constant interaction enables coaches to have firsthand knowledge of the kinds of comprehension instruction teachers practice.

Second, the coach should question teachers—in an unintimidating way—about what they know, what they want to know, and how they want to learn it. A strong relationship of trust between the coach and teachers will aid in this information-gathering process. If you are new or have not yet developed a culture of trust, teachers may be reluctant or resistant to admit what they do not know.

Finally, to determine whether the existing comprehension instruction is effective, the literacy coach must turn to test scores on a variety of assessments that try to measure understanding. Keep in mind that test scores may not always accurately reflect the level of student understanding. Comprehension appears to be much harder to assess than skills such as word knowledge or phonics.

To help you assess teachers' current level of knowledge, ask them to complete a written survey that rates their degree of knowledge of a set of comprehension strategies identified as best practices. Although the responses on the Comprehension Strategies Use Assessment will be colored by the relationship you have with teachers, it is a good way to begin and complements the information from the other prongs.

PART 2

GOALS

- To assist teachers to reflect on their knowledge of comprehension strategies.
- To look for trends across grade levels or within grade levels.
- To inform differentiated professional development plans.
- To set the stage to provide coaching cycles.

IMPLEMENTATION

1. Introduce the Comprehension Strategies Use Assessment at an all-school or grade-level meeting (see "Organizing Grade-Level and Department Meetings" on page 188).

2. Explain that you are planning to differentiate professional development based on need by initiating coaching cycles, learning groups, book clubs (see "Forming a Teacher Book Club" on page 196), and so forth.

3. Distribute forms and give the teachers two to three days to fill out and return them. Another option, if there is already a strong relationship of trust in the school, is to have teachers fill out the form at the same meeting in which you introduce it and to complete and return the forms immediately.

4. Study the completed forms carefully, looking for

    - comprehension strategies that almost everyone is using frequently
    - comprehension strategies that are unknown to almost everyone
    - trends that indicate people are relying largely on a few strategies

5. Prioritize what you see as the strongest areas of need based on strategies that are used infrequently yet are highlighted in your school's curriculum. For example, *synthesize* is written into the 5th grade curriculum, but three out of four 5th grade teaches marked is as an unknown term.

6. Begin to develop coaching options from which teachers can choose, such as all-school presentations, study groups (see "Planning a Teachers' Study Group" on page 192), book clubs, and coaching cycles.

7. Consider giving an all-school presentation to inform people about strategies that appear to be unknown (see "Planning a Professional Development Workshop" on page 36).

REFLECTION, EVALUATION, AND PLANNING

1. As you analyze the survey, which strategies do teachers seem to overuse? What forms of development would the staff need to stretch teachers to employ new strategies? Carefully note any trends in certain grade levels or content areas that diverge from your school's vision for comprehension instruction.

2. Which important strategies go largely unused? What is your plan for breaking down these strategies in ways that make them easier to teach?

3. How do the results of this survey compare with scores on comprehension assessments?

4. Which materials in your professional library best support the professional development of your targeted strategies? What is your plan to add resources where needed?

Comprehension Strategies Use Assessment

Indicate the frequency with which you model, use, or explicitly teach the following comprehension strategies in your classroom. Check "Not Sure" if you are not familiar with the term.

Name _____ Date _____

Comprehension Strategy	Frequently	Sometimes	Rarely	Never	Not Sure
1. Think-Alouds					
2. Text-to-Text Connections					
3. Text-to-World Connections					
4. Text-to-Self Connections					
5. Schema					
6. Prediction					
7. Determining Importance (Fiction)					
8. Determining Importance (Nonfiction)					
9. Visualizing					
10. Synthesizing					
11. QAR (Questioning)					
12. Summarizing					
13. Story Maps					
14. Inferring					
15. DR-TA (Comprehension Monitoring)					
16. Fix-Up Strategies					

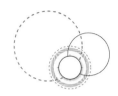

Taking a Running Record

TARGET
Elementary ✓   Middle School/High School __

Teachers have always wanted a way to document how a student reads, and although it is possible to record a child's reading on audiotape or videotape, that solution is unreasonable considering how many students are in an average classroom. Another method is to make a written representation of the child's reading, commonly known as a *running record.*

Originally called *oral reading records,* running records can help teachers identify the current reading level of their students. To take a running record, the teacher sits next to a student, listens to the student read, and quickly and efficiently records the student's reading fluency using a series of checks, miscued words, and other symbols. (For an in-depth review of running records, see the references for further learning below.) Running records use a finely tuned set of books leveled from A through Z according to difficulty. (Books leveled A through I are generally thought to be at 1st grade reading level, J through M are 2nd grade level, N through P are 3rd grade level, and so forth.)

Teachers, alone or in partnership with a literacy coach, can study the written running records to better understand what students know, how they use that knowledge, and what they still need to learn. Running records can also provide teachers with data for grouping students by reading level and determining the difficulty of text appropriate for the reading groups. Finally, they can serve as a way to record individual students' changes and progress over time.

Running records and other documents, such as Reading Level Monitoring Forms (see "Appropriately Grouping Students" on page 81) and records of reading groups, can provide pivotal information that can guide teachers' decisions—as long they are organized in a logical way. One popular method is an assessment notebook, a three-ring binder with a section for each child and a section for the class as a whole. An assessment notebook can help teachers track students' progress over time, provide rich information to share at a parent-teacher conference, and determine whether students are making adequate progress.

There are many different types of running record forms, and the following Informal Running Record Form is only one example of a system that teachers can use to check for fluency. Regardless of the form you adopt, consistency across the school is important because people other than the teacher may need to look at the form to ascertain a student's fluency. A literacy coach might consider devoting time at a grade-level meeting to taking running records.

References for further learning

Clay, M. (2007). *An observation of early literacy achievement.* Portsmouth, NH: Heinemann.

Fountas, I. C., & Pinnell, G. S. (2005). *The Fountas & Pinnell leveled book list, K–8* (2006–2008 ed.). Portsmouth, NH: Heinemann.

GOALS

- To create a written representation of a student's attempt to read a book alone.
- To provide a sample of text reading for the teacher to study and better understand the student's current level of literacy development and the instruction needed to move the student forward.
- To help the teacher match students with others who have similar strengths and needs for small-group or guided-reading instruction.
- To suggest what level of books the teacher should use for the student's reading instruction.
- To document students' progress over a given period of time.

IMPLEMENTATION

1. Show teachers how to take a running record. Remind them that students don't have to read a whole book, just enough to get a picture of the child's reading. They should include page numbers in case they need to do a more in-depth analysis of the running record. If you plan to use the attached form, direct teachers to

   - Mark a check for each accurate word, a long dash for each skipped word, and the word itself if a student substitutes the wrong word.
   - Write down the number of running words (RW) in the text.
   - Count the number of errors, which include word substitutions, word omissions, word insertions, and any words the teacher has to read to the student.
   - Calculate the accuracy using the following formula:

$$\left(\frac{RW - Errors}{RW} \right) 100 = \text{Percent Accuracy}$$

2. Based on the accuracy percentages, help teachers plan what actions they will take, such as changing the student's reading group or book level.

3. Meet with the teacher to analyze the running records to look for patterns in student and group performance and for class trends. For example:

   - Examine a student's running records over a period of time. Is there a pattern in the kinds of behaviors the child exhibits?
   - Compare a proficient reader to a struggling reader. What are the differences in their reading behaviors?
   - Are there patterns in the reading behaviors of ELL students?
   - Look at the running records of four random students in a class. Do they reveal a pattern in the teaching emphasis? Does the teacher need to shift emphases? How will you help implement that shift?

4. Help teachers plan the most efficient routine for administering running records. Some teachers take one brief running record per day by having one student read a short passage by himself after his guided-reading group. Other teachers take a running record of each student every couple of weeks by listening to students read aloud within the small-group setting.

5. Suggest that the teacher keep a stack of Informal Running Record Forms in the guided-reading area to easily transition from working with a group to taking a running record. Keeping running records should only take a few minutes per day if the forms and the books are within easy reach.

6. At the end of one semester, meet with the teacher to evaluate the reading behaviors of an individual student across time. Based on a student's set of running records, what is the student's instructional level? What is the student's fluency level? How does the student's reading behavior change when reading informational text as opposed to narrative text? What is the student's rate of self-correction? What kinds of miscues does the student make?

7. Encourage teachers to share running records data with each other. Some choose one or two students at various levels of expertise and discuss their running records once a month with teammates.

REFLECTION, EVALUATION, AND PLANNING

1. How do teachers respond to using running records? Do their reactions suggest possible topics for professional development? Or would teachers with similar needs or interests be good candidates for a study group?

2. How often are teachers collecting running records? Discuss whether they need to take the same number of running records for all students or whether they need to more carefully monitor some students' progress.

3. How are teachers organizing the record keeping for these forms? Are they keeping assessment notebooks?

4. How are teachers analyzing the data from their students' running records? If they analyze alone, can you encourage them to use grade-level meetings to assess individual student progress as well as progress within the classroom and across grades?

Informal Running Record Form

Date _____ Book Title _____ (pp. ____ to ____) Book Level _____

RW _____ Errors _____ Accuracy % _____ Action _____

- -

Date _____ Book Title _____ (pp. ____ to ____) Book Level _____

RW _____ Errors _____ Accuracy % _____ Action _____

Source: Adapted with permission from the work of Evelyn Acevedo-Nolfi, literacy coach at Avondale School, Chicago, Ill.

Example Informal Running Record

Date 10/1/08   **Book Title** Joshua James Just Likes Trucks   **(pp.** 4 **to** 21 **) Book Level** C

4. ✓ ✓ ✓ ✓

5. ✓ ✓

6. ✓ ✓

9. ✓ ✓

11. Shiny ✓

13. ✓ ✓ _____ ✓ ✓

14. ✓ ✓

15. ✓ ✓

16. ✓ ✓

19. ✓ ✓

21. ✓ _____ ✓ ✓

RW 29   **Errors** 3   **Accuracy %** 90%   **Action** Work on monitoring for self-corrections

Source: Adapted with permission from the work of Evelyn Acevedo-Nolfi, literacy coach at Avondale School, Chicago, Ill.

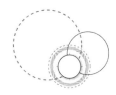

Appropriately Grouping Students

TARGET
Elementary ✓   Middle School/High School ___

When teachers work with students in guided-reading groups, they can tailor literacy instruction to students' individual strengths and needs. One of the tenets of guided reading is dynamic grouping. Students' placement in reading groups should shift frequently based on their most recent running record data. Whenever teachers take a new set of running records (see "Taking a Running Record" on page 75), they should reassess how they've grouped students.

Running records help teachers determine the instructional level of each student. A publisher-produced informal reading inventory—a set of graded texts that calculate the level closest to students' reading ability—serves the same function. After establishing a reading level, the teacher creates guided-reading groups of students who can read at approximately the same level.

The Reading Level Monitoring Form gives teachers a way to organize running record data so that they can easily compare students' reading levels for grouping. It also records how many levels students have moved through in a quarter or a semester, which can spotlight students who need acceleration. The literacy coach can then meet with the teacher to develop an acceleration plan, such as increasing the number of guided-reading sessions per week or forming an after-lunch bunch.

Although conventional wisdom dictates that students should be grouped according to their instructional levels, a study of running records can also yield data about what reading strategies students use. A literacy coach might support a teacher in providing instruction to a mixed-level group who use the same reading strategies. By using a multilevel book, the teacher can support students in developing a specific strategy. When students have achieved the strategy goal, they can return to instructional-level groups.

If the running records aren't resulting in grouping changes, ask the teacher to reflect on the instructional practices that might be contributing to the stagnate groups. You can troubleshoot by referring to the teachers' past guided-reading plans (see "Guiding a Small-Group Reading Lesson" on page 124).

ASCD   ☐ 81

GOALS

- To organize data on which teachers can base guided-reading grouping decisions.
- To track students' reading progress over time.
- To help teachers identify students who need acceleration.

IMPLEMENTATION

1. Set up the Reading Level Monitoring Form by filling in the reading level headings with the range of letters for the teacher's grade level (see "Taking a Running Record" on page 75). Consider including at least one letter above and below the standard reading level range for students who are struggling or excelling. Distribute the customized charts to the teachers.

2. Instruct teachers on how to use the Reading Level Monitoring Form:

    - Based on the running records, highlight the row for each student to the column that corresponds with the student's current reading level.
    - As students progress over time, extend the shading to the appropriate level.

3. Using a sample form, show teachers how they can apply that information to organize groups for guided reading and to help instruction and student evaluation.

REFLECTION, EVALUATION, AND PLANNING

1. What are teachers' reactions to the Reading Level Monitoring Form? Did it make them aware of any trends they hadn't recognized before?

2. When teachers change students' book levels or groups, how do they explain those decisions? Do they use running records to drive their choices?

3. What other kinds of assessments might teachers also need to help them group students for guided reading?

4. How often are teachers changing their reading groups? Do they need to take running records more often or find another way to group students?

Reading Level Monitoring Form

Teacher Name _____ Grade _____ Date: From _____ to _____

Reading Level														
1.														
2.														
3.														
4.														
5.														
6.														
7.														
8.														
9.														
10.														
11.														
12.														
13.														
14.														
15.														
16.														
17.														
18.														
19.														
20.														
21.														
22.														
23.														
24.														
25.														
26.														
27.														
28.														
29.														
30.														

PART 2

Example Reading Level Monitoring Form

Teacher Name __Ms. Sims_____ Grade __1__ Date: From __9-19-08__ to __2-10-09__

Reading Level	A	B	C	D	E	F	G	H	I	J	K	L	M	N
1. Ames, Kevin	▓	▓	▓	▓	▓	▓								
2. Ardmore, Jessica	▓	▓	▓	▓	▓	▓								
3. Cline, Douglas	▓	▓	▓	▓		▓								
4. Coughlin, Katie	▓	▓	▓	▓	▓	▓	▓							
5. Evans, Krysta	▓	▓	▓											
6. Fernandez, Maribel	▓	▓	▓	▓	▓	▓	▓							
7. Guzman, David	▓	▓	▓											
8. Harris, Calvin	▓	▓	▓											
9. Jonas, Allison	▓	▓	▓	▓	▓	▓	▓							
10. King, Gregory	▓	▓												
11. Landman, Olivia	▓	▓	▓	▓	▓	▓	▓	▓	▓	▓				
12. Lawson, Abby	▓	▓	▓	▓	▓									
13. Munoz, Jose	▓	▓	▓	▓										
14. Norris, Timothy	▓	▓	▓	▓		▓								
15. Olson, Irina	▓	▓	▓	▓		▓								
16. Payton, Penny	▓	▓	▓	▓	▓									
17. Pullman, Brian	▓	▓	▓	▓	▓	▓	▓	▓	▓	▓				
18. Ramos, Manuel	▓	▓	▓	▓	▓	▓								
19. Sampson, Michael	▓	▓	▓											
20. Silvers, Pamela	▓	▓	▓	▓										
21. Tyler, Tommy	▓	▓	▓	▓	▓	▓								
22. Williams, Mindy	▓	▓	▓		▓									
23. Wilson, Larry	▓	▓	▓	▓	▓	▓	▓							
24. Yancy, Suzanne	▓	▓	▓	▓										

Reading Groups __2/11__

Olivia	Manuel
Maribel	Tommy
Brian	Abby
Katie	Irina
Larry	Douglas
Allison	Timothy
Jose	Mindy
Pamela	David
Suzanne	Calvin
Kevin	Krysta
Jessica	Michael
Penny	Gregory

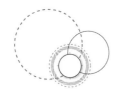

Introducing the Assessment Wall

TARGET

Elementary ✓   Middle School/High School __

An assessment wall is a visual representation of the reading levels of each student. Some assessment walls only document the reading levels of a classroom; others include all classes at a grade level. An ambitious, highly developed assessment wall can document the individual reading levels of children from all classrooms across multiple grade levels.

To construct an assessment wall, teachers first select a standardized way to determine the reading level of each child. The most efficient way is to give each child a running record (see "Taking a Running Record" on page 75) at the beginning of the year and then monthly throughout the school year. By using a finely tuned set of books leveled from A through Z according to difficulty, teachers can identify where students are reading and more sensitively than by using basal levels. Books leveled A through I are generally thought to be at 1st grade reading level, J through M are 2nd grade level, N through P are 3rd grade level, and so forth.

The alphabetical reading levels are posted in a row across the top of an assessment wall, which can be a simple set of pocket charts or a bullet board for teachers to organize cards with students' names. Teachers place students' cards under the letter that matches their performance on the most recent running record. Over time, the cards progress from left to right as students' running records show that they can handle increasingly difficult levels of text.

Although each card represents an individual student, the aim of the assessment wall is to note and track trends across groups of children and across levels. Literacy coaches can help teachers set up the assessment wall; demonstrate how to take the running records; and set up a structured time, usually once a month, to shift the cards.

However, the literacy coach's most critical role is to facilitate teachers' discussion of running records and what those results mean to the organization of names on the assessment wall. The Looking Closely: Discussing the Assessment Wall tool can provide a starting point for your discussion with teachers.

To learn about how you can make an assessment wall even more valuable to teachers, see "Monitoring Progress with the Assessment Wall" on page 92.

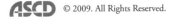

Reference for further learning

Fountas, I. C., & Pinnell, G. S. (2005). *The Fountas & Pinnell leveled book list, K–8* (2006–2008 ed.). Portsmouth, NH: Heinemann.

GOALS

- To encourage teachers to use informal running records to monitor reading levels.
- To promote productive grade-level discussions about reading level patterns within and across grade levels through studying the assessment wall.
- To prompt rich discussions about the classroom instruction and curriculum needs of groups of students not progressing.
- To open discussions with administration about the need for external interventions for children who do not respond to good classroom instruction.
- To prompt important discussions about how to meet the needs of students who are either reading at or above grade level.
- To supply information about the number of titles at each book level a classroom needs to best meet the number of students reading at each level.

IMPLEMENTATION

1. Find an out-of-the-way place to hang the pocket charts or a bulletin board to which you can affix a small card for each student. Place cards A through Z across the top row.
2. Consider starting small by finding a willing teacher or grade level to begin the assessment wall. Over time, others may join.
3. After participating teachers become comfortable giving informal running records, distribute 2-inch-by-3-inch cards for them to write the name of each student in their class. Over time, you might decide that the wall's results would be more comprehensive if the cards included other information, such whether students receive special services, are English language learners, or are new to the school.
4. Invite teachers to place their cards in the pocket chart or on the bulletin board prior to the first meeting.
5. Distribute discussion forms to teachers at a grade-level meeting (see "Organizing Grade-Level and Department Meetings" on page 188) next to the wall, and invite teachers to record their impressions.
6. Engage teachers in a conversation about student progress using the form as a reference point.
7. Set short-term goals for next steps and actions items, including a plan to discuss the status of these goals and action items at the next grade-level meeting.

PART 2

REFLECTION, EVALUATION, AND PLANNING

1. How can you guide the discussion about this form to focus on how children learn and instruction related to that learning?

2. What kind of student learning goals and actions came to light during the discussion of this form? If goals are not appropriate, how can you steer the discussion to help?

3. What materials and resources do teachers need to support their goals and actions?

4. Did teacher response to the wall reveal any particular professional development needs?

5. As teachers become comfortable using the assessment wall, how can you work with them to share their work and learning with others in the school?

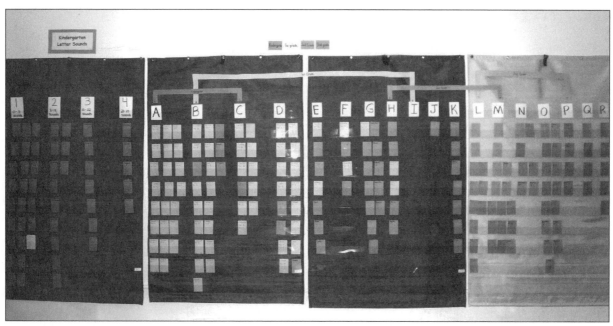

This assessment wall shows the reading levels of students in grades 1–3.

Looking Closely: Discussing the Assessment Wall

1. What do you notice?

2. Which groups of students are at expected levels? What kinds of literacy experiences are promoting this progress? How much are these children reading daily in connected text?

3. Which groups of students are above expected levels? How can we challenge these students? How much are these children reading daily in connected text?

4. Which groups of students are not at expected levels? What additional or different kinds of instruction can we offer these students? How much are these students reading daily in connected text?

Setting a Time Line for Reading-Level Goals

TARGET
Elementary ✓   Middle School/High School __

The assessment wall (see "Introducing the Assessment Wall" on page 85) enables teachers to picture where individual students, as well as the class as a whole, are in terms of reading level at any given time. The end goal, to have all students reading at or above grade level by the end of the year, is clear. But without intermittent reading level targets, how do teachers know whether their students are on track to reach the ultimate grade-level reading goal?

The literacy coach and teachers must first look at the entire school year and set benchmarks for what on-grade-level reading is at certain points. To help set those standards, you can refer to established norms, such as those provided by Gay Su Pinnell and Irene C. Fountas in *The Fountas & Pinnell Leveled Book List, K–8.* For instance, the authors suggest that levels B through H or I are on grade level for students in 1st grade. Once you have identified the end reading level, the literacy coach and the teacher can use what's called *backward planning* to plot what reading levels students should be at during each month.

One group of 2nd grade teachers from a large urban district decided to follow Fountas and Pinnell's suggestion that 2nd graders should cover levels H through M. The literacy coach led them to reflect and map where they expected students to be at a variety of points if they wanted students to be reading at level M at the end of 2nd grade. The teachers in this group came up with this proposal:

Proposal for 2nd Grade

	Sept.	Oct.	Nov.	Dec.	Jan.	Feb.	March	April	May	June
Reading Level	H/I		→ J		→ K		→ L			→ M

Using these benchmarks as at-grade-level reading, the literacy coach led teachers to periodically reflect on whether they were getting their students on or above their grade-level goal.

Working with groups of teachers by grade level, you can use the following Reading Level Time Line to set reading-level targets that teachers can aim for throughout the year.

References for further learning

Dorn, L., & Soffos, S. (2006). *Results that last: A literacy model for school change* [DVD]. Portland, ME: Stenhouse.

Fountas, I. C., & Pinnell, G. S. (2005). *The Fountas & Pinnell leveled book list, K–8* (2006–2008 ed.). Portsmouth, NH: Heinemann.

GOALS

- To set monthly targets for students' reading levels to ensure that they are on track to finish the school year on grade level.
- To help teachers shape their instruction based on forthcoming reading-level goals.

IMPLEMENTATION

1. After teachers become familiar with managing the assessment wall, lead them in a discussion about where students should be at each month of the school year. You can begin by asking, "If we want students to be at level _____ at the end of the year, at what point in time would they have to be at the preceding level?" This may be most clear for 1st through 3rd grade students.

2. Make sure teachers are leaving adequate time to move students forward at the end of the year. Some teachers tend to allow more time at the beginning of the year to get through easier levels.

3. While creating this time line, remind teachers that they are establishing an expectation and not documenting the norm—where most students happen to be at those points in time.

4. Give all the teachers a copy of the time line so that they can refer to the benchmark dates and levels and plan or modify their instruction accordingly.

REFLECTION, EVALUATION, AND PLANNING

1. How are teachers explaining the difference between a reading level norm (where most students are situated) and a reading level expectation (where they hope students will be)? What professional development can you provide that will increase their understanding about the differences between the two?

2. Did teachers at certain grade levels struggle to set targets more than others? How can you anticipate such challenges in the future?

Reading Level Time Line

Proposal for __ Grade

	Sept.	Oct.	Nov.	Dec.	Jan.	Feb.	March	April	May	June
Reading Level										

Monitoring Progress with the Assessment Wall

TARGET
Elementary ✓   Middle School/High School __

Literacy coaches can make an assessment wall, a visual representation of the reading levels of each student (see "Introducing the Assessment Wall" on page 85), even more valuable by helping teachers analyze the progress represented on the wall over time. By being able to accurately interpret the wall, teachers can judge whether their students are on track.

Each time teachers reassess their students, they change the position of the students' cards on the assessment wall. An important service the literacy coach can provide is to collect the data and then show teachers how the students are distributed, calculating what percentage of students have reached the target of on-grade-level reading for that time period. The coach interprets the students' progress based on their position on the assessment wall and the monthly targets on the teacher's Reading Level Time Line (See "Setting a Time Line for Reading-Level Goals" on page 89).

Literacy coaches periodically tally how many students are at each level and tabulate the percent of students who are on grade level according to the proposed time line. Teachers can use this data to modify their instruction techniques to usher more students toward grade-level reading.

Some coaches prepare a chart for each month or each time the assessment wall is changed. The beginning and middle of the school year are especially important points in time because teachers still have time to change their instruction before the end of the year.

Reference for further learning

Dorn, L., & Soffos, S. (2006). *Results that last: A literacy model for school change* [DVD]. Portland, ME: Stenhouse.

GOALS

- To analyze the assessment wall for changes over time.
- To decide whether students reading below grade level are making the kind of progress that allows them to catch up.

- To document whether the percentage of students reading below or on grade level changes over time.

IMPLEMENTATION

1. Record the number of students at each reading level.
2. Compare the chart to the time line of reading levels that you agreed on, and based on the date, highlight the cells at and above the on-grade-level reading column.
3. Count the total number of students on the chart, and then figure the percentage of students at each level.
4. Share these percentage charts with teachers to help them decide on a course of action, especially for those students who seem to remain below grade-level reading levels. Use this data to support discussion when you and teachers change or analyze the assessment wall.

REFLECTION, EVALUATION, AND PLANNING

1. Did certain teachers seem to better understand the notion of accelerating students? Can you encourage them to share with other teachers how the charts might guide plans to help their students catch up? This kind of teacher sharing may be more powerful than coaching advice.
2. Students who are "on the bubble" are reading slightly below expected levels. Often, a little boost is enough to get the students where they need to be. These students are good candidates for short-term support, which often results in a quick win. Can you identify any borderline students? What techniques might you suggest to the teacher to get them reading at grade level?
3. After discussing student growth using the information on the assessment wall, teachers might decide to make some adjustments in the instructional program for some students. They may increase the number of guided reading periods each week, change instructional materials, or change the focus of instruction. To evaluate the effectiveness of instructional change, revisit prior assessment wall data and compare it to current data. Did the treatment have any effect on student growth?
4. Assessment wall data allows you to identify the times of year when progress seems to slow down. Is it before or after a vacation? Is it after standardized testing? Make teachers aware of the phenomenon so that they can increase their level of vigilance during these periods to ensure that the instructional program stays on track.
5. Are you keeping organized records of assessment wall data? By maintaining assessment wall data over the years, you can track the progress of students across grades.

Charts for Calculating Percentages of Students at Each Reading Level

Percentages 1st Graders at each Level

Date	A	B	C	D	E	F	G	H/H+	Percent reading at or above grade level

Percentages 2nd Graders at each Level

Date	Below H	H/I	J	K	L	M/M+	Percent reading at or above grade level

Percentages 3rd Graders at each Level

Date	Below N	N	O	P/P+	Percent reading at or above grade level

Example Charts for Calculating Percentages of Students at Each Reading Level

▓▓▓ = At or above grade level at that point in time according to expectations established by teachers on the reading level time line

Percentages 1st Graders at each Level

Date	A	B	C	D	E	F	G	H or H+	Percent reading at or above grade level
10/10/07	15	13	21	28	10	2	0	10	22%
2/22/08		14	10	18	11	9	6	31	46%
6/10/08				8		14	7	70	70%

▓▓▓ = At or above grade level at that point in time according to expectations established by teachers on the reading level time line

Percentages 2nd Graders at each Level

Date	Below H	H/I	J	K	L	M/M+	Percent reading at or above grade level
9/14/07	24	50	15	10			75%
1/30/08	9	10	10	50	10	10	70%
5/15/08		5	10	20		70	70%

Taking a Fluency Snapshot

TARGET
Elementary ✓   Middle School/High School ✓

At the start of the school year, or whenever teachers are meeting a new group of students, they benefit from having a quick snapshot of the reading levels of a class to establish starting points for more detailed reflection. Just as a class picture on the first day of school can help them learn their students' names and faces and give them an initial point of reference, a classroom fluency snapshot (CFS) can help them get a sense of the literacy level of the class.

The CFS is curriculum-based because the teacher uses a piece of ordinary classroom text to collect a short sample of each student's oral reading. To measure fluency, a CFS uses correct words per minute, or how accurately a student reads a particular passage at a good rate and with prosody (sounds like language).

Fluency strongly correlates with comprehension, and a fluency measure can show whether students can handle the word level and prosody demands of a text. However, this type of assessment is meant to supplement, not to substitute for, richer data collected anecdotally and through other authentic means throughout the year.

Although fluency can also be measured with more detail on an informal reading inventory and in running records (see "Taking a Running Record" on page 75), they are also more labor intensive. If teachers need a quick impression to guide later, more detailed assessment, a CFS is a good option. Once they have gathered the CFS, teachers can create a classroom fluency grid to see the range of fluency and compare students' levels over time. The following Example Fluency Snapshot Grid was prepared for a 2nd grade classroom, but you can modify the range of correct words per minute to customize the grid for teachers' grade levels. For guidelines on standard rates of correct words per minute for different grades, see *Reading Diagnosis for Teachers: An Instructional Approach* (Barr, Blachowicz, Katz, & Kaufman, 2007).

It may be helpful to introduce the classroom fluency grid to a group of teachers by modeling it at an inservice workshop (see "Planning a Professional Development Workshop" on page 36). Have teachers work with partners calculate to their correct words per minutes on a selection from an adult-level narrative textbook. Because they are good readers, ask them to make a few errors on purpose. After teachers have set up the fluency grid, you can use the Teacher's Think Sheet: Interpreting a Classroom Fluency Grid (see page 104) to help them learn how to use the assessment to inform instruction.

References for further learning

Barr, R., Blachowicz, C. L. Z., Katz, C., & Kaufman, B. (2007). *Reading diagnosis for teachers: An instructional approach* (5th ed.). White Plains, NY: Longman.

Blachowicz, C. L. Z., Sullivan, D., & Cieply, C. (2001). Fluency snapshots: A quick screening tool for your classroom. *Reading Psychology, 22*(2), 83–94.

GOALS

- To help teachers get a quick sense of the class baseline at the beginning of the school year.
- To identify students who may need special support or more time when working with grade-level material.
- To help teachers select independent reading material.
- To enable teachers to chart the progress of students' fluency over the year as a measure of overall progress.

IMPLEMENTATION

1. Ask teachers to have each student read a selection from a standard classroom text for one minute. Teachers can time the reading with a stopwatch. Direct them to note how many errors each student makes and how long each student took to read the selection.
2. Provide teachers with the following formula to calculate each student's correct words per minute:

$$\frac{\text{Total number of words} - \text{errors}}{\text{Minutes read}} = \text{Correct words per minute}$$

3. Instruct the teacher to write each student's name and score on a sticky note.
4. Provide the teacher with a vertical snapshot grid, modifying the following template with the range of numbers for the teacher's grade level. Highlight the range that indicates a typical reading range for students in the grade.
5. Ask the teacher to place the sticky notes along the continuum.

PART 2

6. As you work with the teacher, some of the following questions will be helpful to prompt discussions:

- What are the characteristics of a good selection to use for fluency assessment?
- What language should be used in introducing this to your students?
- How can you end the session making sure each student feels affirmed?
- What should you do if you know this text will be too difficult for some students?
- When would it be useful to create such a grid?
- What conclusions can you draw from a completed fluency grid?
- What do you learn about your students from a fluency measure?
- What are the cautions about using this process?

REFLECTION, EVALUATION, AND PLANNING

1. How will you do a modeling session?
2. Based on the inservice training, do any teachers need more preparation before working with students?
3. How will you monitor the teachers' progress on the snapshots?
4. When is the right time for an interpretation meeting?
5. What resources can you make available for appropriate text selection?
6. Which teachers need clocks or stopwatches?

Fluency Snapshot Grid

To calculate correct words per minute, use the following equation:

$$\frac{\text{Total number of words} - \text{errors}}{\text{Minutes read}} = \text{Correct words per minute}$$

Correct Words
Per Minute

140
135
130
125
120
115
110
105
100
95
90
85
80
75
70
65
60
55
50
45
40
35
30
25

Shading indicates typical oral reading rates for 2nd graders as indicated in *Reading Diagnosis for Teachers: An Instructional Approach* (Barr, Blachowicz, Katz, & Kaufman, 2007, p. 25).

Example Fluency Snapshot Grid

Reading in September 2001	Correct Words Per Minute	Reading in January 2002
Katie (158)	160	Jeb (172)
	155	
	150	Mary (146)
	145	Katie (143)
Mary (136)	140	
	135	
Andy (127)	130	
	125	Haley (123)
	120	Andy (121)
	115	
	110	
	105	
Haley (96)	100	Louis (99) Neal (99)
	95	
Chuck (90)	90	Chuck (91)
	85	Barbara (89) Kathy (86)
Emily (80)	80	Catherine (84)
Kathy (76)	75	
Jeb (73) Barbara (73)	70	Emily (72)
		Jenny (68)
Louis (67)	65	Nancy (67)
		Pablo (63) Richard (63)
Catherine (59) Neal (59)	60	Alison (60)
Nancy (54)	55	
Jenny (52)	50	
Alison (45)	45	
	40	
	35	
Pablo (31)	30	
Richard (26)	25	
	20	
	15	

Interpreting a Classroom Fluency Grid

TARGET

Elementary ✔   Middle School/High School ✔

After the literacy coach has introduced classroom fluency snapshots to teachers (see "Taking a Fluency Snapshot" on page 96) and they have filled in their first classroom fluency grids, some of the coach's most important and complex work begins: to move teachers from assessment to data to instruction. This journey involves using assessment formatively, which allows teachers to use data to make informed decisions about instruction, curriculum, and grouping in the future.

A classroom fluency snapshot helps teachers measure students' correct words per minute, and a fluency grid organizes the scores of the whole class as the first step to assessing the data. The literacy coach must consider how to help teachers use the data in ways that let them make good decisions.

Coaches know that the power of assessments is lost if teachers only administer them and file them away or submit them to administrators. To move teachers toward planning and forward thinking, you can encourage reflection and planning by asking questions about the classroom fluency grid:

- How are we doing?
- What are we doing best?
- What do these assessments measure?
- What are we missing?
- Is this the best we can do?
- Where should we place more emphasis?
- What do we already do that we can do more of?
- Is there something we can do sooner in the year?
- Where can we place less emphasis?

Bringing together teachers to discuss and interpret the information from their fluency grids will foster an atmosphere of collaboration and sharing as well as keep teachers informed about fluency across grade levels. Literacy coaches can prompt these meetings and jumpstart discussion with the following Teacher's Think Sheet. If you are working with only one teacher, you can adapt the steps to accommodate a one-on-one partnership.

Reference for further learning

Buhle, R., & Blachowicz, C. (2008, December–2009, January). The assessment double play. *Educational Leadership, 66*(4), 42–46.

GOALS

- To study the range of fluency in a classroom.
- To provide information to group students for instruction.
- To discuss the relationship between a student's rate and the materials the student is given to read.
- To identify instructional settings that might help students improve their fluency.

IMPLEMENTATION

1. Arrange a meeting and have teachers bring in their class fluency grids (see "Taking a Fluency Snapshot" on page 96).

2. Have teachers pair up for a Think, Pair, Share to examine an example grid and discuss what they see. Ask them to reflect on

    - What the assessments are measuring.
    - How students are doing with fluency.
    - The best fluency that could be achieved with this class.
    - The kinds of instruction or practice opportunities the class could benefit from.
    - What the teacher of this class might begin sooner in the year.
    - Whether the teacher is emphasizing a technique that doesn't support fluency.

3. Have them generate insights and questions about the grid.

4. After working with the example and reflecting in a large group, ask them to work in grade-level groups to use the interpretation think sheet to understand their own classroom data.

5. Bring the teachers back together to debrief on their conclusions as a group.

REFLECTION, EVALUATION, AND PLANNING

1. Did teachers seem to understand what was being measured and what was not being measured? If not, what help will they need to see the relationship between these scores and instructional decisions?

2. Which group of students seemed to stand out as having clear-cut strengths and needs? What group of students' results did not match the teachers' expectations?

3. What kind of support are teachers planning to offer to accelerate fluency in the classroom? What professional development can you provide to make sure that they know the most effective actions to take? What resources do they need to accelerate students?

4. Do any teachers seem willing to delve deeper and form a study group (see "Planning a Teachers' Study Group" on page 192) about improving fluency?

5. If you only met with a limited number of teachers, are any willing to share their findings and plans with other staff?

Teacher's Think Sheet: Interpreting a Classroom Fluency Grid

1. Which of your students displayed high reading fluency and might need more of a challenge? How will you challenge them in whole-class work?

2. Which of your students might have trouble with grade-level texts? Looking at their performance, can you tell what type of supplementary work they will need? How will you support them with whole-class work?

3. Of your average performers, is there anyone who concerns you? Did you notice anything specific about their reading, such as accurate, inaccurate, slow, speedy, phrasing, or sounds they did or did not understand?

4. Beyond helping with grouping, how will you use these data to guide your instruction other than what you have noted above?

Analyzing Your Instruction

TARGET
Elementary ✓   Middle School/High School ✓

Making the most out of a typical 90–120 minute literacy block has become the mission—and challenge—of classroom teachers. They know that the decisions they make about how to use that time will have a profound effect on student achievement. With the help of the Practices to Increase and Practices to Decrease charts, the literacy coach can structure a conversation with teachers about their instructional decisions during the literacy block.

These tools and the ensuing discussion can help teachers and coaches distinguish current practices that have the potential to make the biggest difference in student achievement. Although we can become wedded to practices that we have used repeatedly and enjoy presenting, everything done in the literacy block must be seen through the lens of its influence on students' literacy learning. For instance, allowing a solid block of time for students to read independently at their own level appears to increase fluency. According to student comments, reading books that are self-selected and at their own reading level gives them a chance to learn what adults know: that reading can be both informational and enjoyable.

Conversely, practices such as always instructing students in a whole-group setting, using the same text for all, can be too easy for some and too difficult for others. The hope is that each school will identify instructional practices that are most likely to make a difference.

The following grids include some practices generally acknowledged as either powerful or not effective at helping children become successfully literate. However, each school may also have a set of practices that are especially important for the students in their population. This is especially clear when a primary building is compared to a middle school setting. The latter may require additional practices specifically targeted to supporting the amount of content-area reading that middle school students are given.

It becomes one of the important jobs of the literacy coach to help teachers develop these lists, to reflect and understand why some practices are more powerful, and to provide the staff development needed to implement them.

PART 2

GOALS

- To closely examine current literacy instruction practices.
- To identify practices currently in place that facilitate student achievement.
- To identify current practices that have a negligible influence on student achievement.
- To support teachers to increase best practice instructional strategies.

IMPLEMENTATION

1. Decide whether you want to use one or both forms provided. Study the practices listed on both of these sheets to see whether they fit the curriculum and values of your school. If necessary, add practices that are important to your school.
2. Decide whether these forms would be more effective as a whole-school activity or whether you should target a grade level or small group of teachers across grade levels. Consider your schedule and decide whether starting with a small group would be more manageable and effective.
3. Plan an inservice workshop so that teachers can talk about each practice listed. Clarify and answer questions, using this discussion to get a sense of what professional development teachers may need.
4. Let teachers work individually, in pairs, or in grade-level groups to fill out the forms. The more actively involved they are in evaluating their practices, the more likely they are to commit to change.
5. Collect the grids and chart your next steps as a literacy coach, including how you will use schoolwide professional development, study groups (see "Planning a Teachers' Study Group" on page 192), and coaching cycles (see "The Coaching Cycle" on page 54). Be ready to explain your time constraints so that teachers have reasonable expectations. Consider asking teachers to prioritize their wish lists.
6. Share plans with teachers.

REFLECTION, EVALUATION, AND PLANNING

1. How did teachers respond to the completed grids?
2. Which nonrecommended practice is the most prevalent? Which recommended practice is the most prevalent?
3. Which practice will require the most support to initiate?
4. What materials do teachers need to support the recommended practices?
5. Which teachers are willing to demonstrate recommended practices? Are they willing to share with their colleagues? Would videotaping be a less threatening way to share?

6. Which books in your professional library best support the implementation of recommended practices? Construct a list of books to add to the library.

7. Which strategies interest multiple teachers, suggesting the possibility of beginning a study group?

8. Which one critical instructional practice lends itself to an all-school professional development session that you can follow up with small-group work with a targeted group of teachers?

9. To gather pre- and post-information about any strategy inservice training you provide, consider introducing the grids at set times in the year.

PART 2

Practices to Increase

Practice	Where are you now?	When can you implement the practice?	What barriers might prevent implementation?	What supports are needed to implement the practice?
Read aloud 3–6 times daily				
Independent-level reading time daily for all students				
Meet daily with 2–3 instructional level guided-reading groups; meet with struggling readers every day				
Word study connected to actual reading and writing				
Students engaged in daily connected writing (e.g., writing workshop)				
Explicit instruction in comprehension and vocabulary with time for students to talk to each other				

Practices to Decrease

Practice	Where are you now?	When do you expect to eliminate the practice?	What might you use to replace it?	What do you need to help you replace the practice?
Morning Story or other forms of work that let students copy rather than compose				
Only whole-class reading instruction				
Students regularly instructed above or below their instructional level				
Regular and routine use of workbook pages and worksheets instead in reading and content areas				
Only teacher-directed questions, without opportunities for students to talk to each other				
Discrete instruction that does not include attempts to integrate units				

Analyzing Your Word Wall

TARGET
Elementary ✓   Middle School/High School ✓

In many classrooms, the word wall is a staple. The word wall is designed to help students develop sight word and writing vocabularies and to support instruction. To create the wall, teachers choose high-frequency words and systematically add words each week as they engage students in activities that direct their attention to the word wall.

The most important factor in the effectiveness of the word wall is the selection of the words. The words need to fulfill two requirements: (1) students at a particular grade level use them frequently across all writing activities and (2) they can be used to build similarly spelled words. For instance, the word *that* would be a good choice because young children frequently use it in their writing. It's also a good word because it contains the word family *–at*. The teacher can use *that* to help students build similarly spelled words, such as *sat* and *flat*.

When all the students in a class have mastered a word on the wall, teachers remove that word. When used effectively, word walls can be a valuable classroom asset. They can support student writing, provide practice for sight word retention, and offer models for word analysis.

Literacy teachers should make sure that teachers truly understand the principles and recommended practices of word walls. Unfortunately, it is not uncommon to see word walls containing 100 words posted in a 1st grade classroom during the second week of school. Emphasize that the wall should consist of high-frequency words, such as *like* and *said,* instead of content words, such as *condensation* and *evaporation*. When teachers don't use a word wall appropriately, it's little more than a classroom decoration.

Used appropriately as both a teaching device and a resource for students while they are writing, the word wall can be an excellent way to combine phonics and writing instruction with real-life reading and writing. Literacy coaches can help teachers assess the effectiveness of their word walls by distributing and then discussing the Evaluating Your Word Wall survey at a meeting of teachers in the same grade level or across grade levels.

It may be necessary for the literacy coach to provide word wall applications beyond the early elementary grades. Teachers in the late elementary, middle school, and high school level have sometimes opted to incorporate word walls in their instruction. You might recommend this application to teachers who are looking for new ideas to support word learning in higher grades. Here are some variations for using word walls:

- English technology teachers can post word walls with the list of words that spell-checker doesn't catch, such as homonyms. Students are cautioned to seek out other sources to verify the spellings of the words on these word walls.
- Foreign language teachers can use word walls in the same way as the primary grades. After all, their students are beginning readers in the foreign language. The word wall activities offer students a break from traditional vocabulary building and keep the words available visually.
- English teachers can create interactive walls by posting their Latin and Greek roots. For example, for the root "graph," the students and teacher define the root and give the origin. The students collect and post words like *graphic, telegraph, autographic, biography, seismograph,* and *polygraph* when they encounter them in their reading and writing.
- Math teachers can use word walls to post keywords for the four basic mathematical operations. Some students' difficulty with math actually stems from vocabulary problems. For example, under the "addition" column, a teacher might post: *sum, total, plus, in all,* and of course the symbol +. ELL students who understand how to do the operation but are stymied by the language find these word walls especially useful.
- Writing teachers can used word walls to help their students make better word choices in writing. Students are encouraged to find precise words to express the meaning of an overused word, such as *happy.*
- ELL students have come to depend on cognates to help them negotiate the second language. Word walls that feature cognates can help these students.

References for further learning

Cunningham, P. M. (2008). *Phonics they use: Words for reading and writing* (5th ed.). Boston: Pearson.

Pinnell, G. S., & Fountas, I. C. (1998). *Word matters: Teaching phonics and spelling in the reading/ writing classroom.* Portsmouth, NH: Heinemann.

GOALS

- To engage teachers in conversations about the effective use of word walls.
- To demonstrate how to use reading, writing, and phonics instruction to support each other.
- To provide a way for literacy coaches to support teachers as they critically analyze their word walls.

IMPLEMENTATION

1. Distribute the word wall evaluation form at a grade-level meeting or a vertical meeting with teachers in grades K–2 (see "Organizing Grade-Level and Department Meetings" on page 188).
2. After they complete the form, engage teachers in a conversation about what is working well with their word walls.
3. Invite teachers to focus on one thing that they might want to change about how they're implementing their word walls.
4. Accept volunteers to visit a laboratory classroom to see word wall activities.
5. Distribute evaluation forms to document how teachers receive this tool.

REFLECTION, EVALUATION, AND PLANNING

1. Which teachers were most receptive to the idea of examining their word wall use? Is there at least one per grade level who can later share her work with teammates?
2. What similarities and differences did you notice between the teachers' analysis of how they use their word walls and your observations of both word walls and the teachers' use of them? Was their assessment different than what you saw, in terms of the word walls themselves and the instruction?
3. What did teachers identify to improve their use of word walls? What role will you play in those changes?
4. How would you describe the teachers' response to this word wall evaluation form? If it was not positive, what can you change to make it more helpful to teachers and to you?
5. Who volunteered to visit laboratory classrooms to see more word wall activities?
6. Do you have the materials you need, such as enough copies of books or articles, to quickly form study groups (see "Planning a Teachers' Study Group" on page 192) or learning groups about word walls after you ask teachers to fill out these evaluation forms?

Evaluating Your Word Wall

Use this checklist to evaluate the placement, structure, and use of your classroom word wall.

- ☐ There are 20–40 words on my classroom word wall (K). There are 100–120 words on my word wall (1,2).
- ☐ I began the school year with a blank word wall.
- ☐ I added the words gradually and systematically over the entire school year.
- ☐ My classroom word wall has high-utility, high-frequency words that my students use in their reading and writing each day.
- ☐ I actively engage my students in word wall activities 2–3 times each week.
- ☐ I incorporate the word wall into general literacy activities (i.e., shared reading, interactive writing, writing workshop, poem of the week).
- ☐ The median child in my classroom can read 80 percent of the words on my classroom word wall.
- ☐ The words on my classroom word walls are written with a thick, black-ink, permanent marker on pieces of colored paper.
- ☐ My classroom word wall is accessible and visible to all children in my classroom.
- ☐ I have removed words as the children have gained proficiency in reading and spelling them.

Changes that I would consider making to my word wall:

Browsing Your Anthology

TARGET

Elementary ✓   Middle School/High School __

Many schools and districts use commercial reading series, which offer easy access to leveled materials and a shared vocabulary and a structure for reading instruction. The teacher's manuals also provide instructional rationales, routines, and professional development information. Though a commercial reading series is not a comprehensive program for literacy, it can be a useful tool, especially for new teachers and teachers new to a grade level.

Commercial reading series are most effective when teachers take the stance of a critical user to decide how to incorporate these materials into their overall plan for literacy and to determine how they align with the school and district's curriculum and philosophy. Because commercial series are full of ideas for literacy, it is also important that teachers are selective and choose tools that work for them, rather than having the teacher work for the tool.

In a school with a core reading program, literacy coaches can use the following worksheet with new teachers or teachers new to a level. Work with teachers to examine—step by step—the materials for their grade level, trying to tease out

- how the materials are organized
- what the unit themes are
- how units are organized
- estimates of the pacing that is suggested by the materials
- the weekly format
- the reading content for the week
- the organization of skills and strategy instruction
- optional instructional features

GOALS

- To demonstrate a process of materials review.
- To familiarize new teachers or teachers new to a grade with the materials that provide continuity across the school.

- To help teachers plan for pacing over the course of a year.
- To help teachers develop a format for weekly planning.
- To understand how to use a core set of materials in a balanced program.
- To determine priorities for selecting or omitting components of anthology lessons.

IMPLEMENTATION

1. Set up a meeting with teachers and ask them to bring a new pupil book and teacher editions.

2. Distribute the Teachers' Core Program Analysis Sheet to each teacher. Let teachers work alone or with a grade-level partner to make a first pass through the sheet. To help shape the discussion, ask

   - Which parts do you consider essential and which discretionary?
   - What will you use as suggested?
   - What will you change or adapt?
   - What kind of help would you like to get started?

REFLECTION, EVALUATION, AND PLANNING

1. Construct a list of materials that teachers still needed.
2. What materials and strategies will teachers need for students who cannot read this text?
3. How will this text support students in each classroom who struggle?
4. Which teachers will need more support starting their planning?
5. How will you keep track of pacing?

Teachers' Core Program Analysis Sheet: Browsing Your Anthology

1. Look at the pupil book. What are the themed units? How many are there?

2. How many subunits are in each themed unit?

3. Look at the unit that represents a week (there are usually 32–38 of these). How many reading selections does it contain? How long is each? Does there appear to be one or more main selection? How does it relate to the others?

4. Analyze the weekly format for the balance among

   - vocabulary and prior knowledge
   - comprehension, fluency, and attention to word study and decoding
   - critical thinking and extension through writing and talk and other media

5. Do students read across texts? What else is there that you want to use? Spelling, writing, oral language? Science, social studies, arts? What will you skip?

6. How will you use this core book in your total program?

7. What other comments or notes do you want to make?

Selecting Leveled Books

TARGET
Elementary ✓   Middle School/High School __

In the last 15 years, small, single-story, carefully leveled "little books" have become an increasingly popular choice for reading instruction in the early elementary grades. Sometimes they replace a traditional basal text. Other times, they enrich a school's existing basal texts to provide more choices for small-group instruction, independent reading, or pull-out intervention programs.

Teachers and literacy coaches who are committed to providing multiple stories each week to struggling students want as many titles as possible. They want their struggling students to have the same volume of connected text as students who are able to read longer stories. These little books can also provide additional, more challenging texts for teachers to use with their most proficient readers. Another important advantage is that little books are sensitively leveled (Fountas & Pinnell, 2008) and can make it easier to match students to the books at just the right level.

Literacy coaches frequently support teachers and administrators in choosing little books. The choice is easier when schools pay extra to buy the little books associated with their basal series. In these cases, the little books are usually coordinated to the basal stories and their level of challenge is clearly identified. Some schools prefer to order little books from publishers who specialize in them. Literacy coaches can obtain catalogues and sample texts and work with teachers to pick ones that meet the needs of targeted groups of students.

The Selecting Little Books K–2 tool gives teachers a sense of the kinds of choices available and provides a structure for thinking about how to make choices. However, because publishing is a dynamic business, it is difficult to provide any kind of complete, up-to-date list that can stand the test of time. This tool is intended to show the kind of thinking and planning literacy coaches can do to help make selection easier for their teachers and administrators. Although in some schools, literacy coaches are asked to choose books by themselves, the steps below are suggested for coaches who collaborate with teachers to make the selections.

This planning becomes more important when teachers at different grade levels, special education staff, ELL teachers, and intervention teachers are all ordering books. Teachers want the text they use to be new to their students, so you should keep track of which teachers will be using which sets and that their selections do not overlap.

Reference for further learning

Fountas, I. C., & Pinnell, G. S. (2005). *The Fountas & Pinnell leveled book list, K–8* (2006–2008 ed.). Portsmouth, NH: Heinemann.

GOALS

- To select little book sets that match the needs of students at each grade level, that lend themselves to small-group instruction, and that provide a continuous stream of levels across grades.
- To provide enough below-, on-, and above-grade-level books to ensure that each teacher can provide a volume of reading opportunities to all groups within the classroom.
- To ensure equal quantities of nonfiction and informational texts.

IMPLEMENTATION

1. Meet with and survey classroom and intervention teachers to find out what levels and kinds of books they need.
2. Review and analyze any existing books in your literacy closet (see "Organizing a Literacy Closet" on page 208).
3. Order catalogues and samples from book distributors.
4. Preselect sets that best match the needs of the school and enter names on a grid, adding notes to help teachers think about the books. You can tailor the Selecting Little Books K–2 grid to match the needs and resources of your school.
5. Arrange to have a book month, during which time you make samples and catalogues available for teachers to peruse and, if possible, take back to their rooms to try with a student.
6. Meet with each grade level to decide which series will be devoted to which grade level or whether one series of little books will work across multiple grade levels.
7. Study the grid to make sure there is cohesion across all grade levels, that quantities ensure enough titles to guarantee adequate reading opportunities for all groups, and that there will not be the chance of duplicating titles across grade levels.

8. If funds do not allow for you to purchase all the books requested, meet with administrators to develop a long-term plan for ordering books during the next two or three years according to prioritized needs. Revisit decisions annually and revise the plan as needed.

REFLECTION, EVALUATION, AND PLANNING

1. If you don't already have a literacy closet to house and share books, what is your plan to begin one?
2. Count the number of books at each level. Construct a wish list to purchase additional titles that support the instructional program at each grade level or the intervention program. You may need to develop a multiyear plan for acquiring all the books.
3. Survey teachers to determine whether the traditional set of six copies per title works effectively for the size of their reading groups. If not, how can you remedy this?
4. If leveled books are the only books teachers use, how will you ensure that students have a sufficient volume of reading?
5. Outline a professional development plan for using the little books for instruction, such as how to introduce books and select vocabulary.

Selecting Little Books K–2

Date Titles Selected _____

Publisher/Series	For K Classrooms	For 1st Grade Classrooms	For 2nd Grade Classrooms	For ELL Classrooms	For Special Ed and Reading Specialist Pullout
RIGBY SAILS *Natural language format but stronger than usual repetition of high-frequency sight words.*					
RIGBY PM READERS *Books with an urban flavor.*					
RIGBY STORY STEPS *Thematically grouped. Includes one benchmark book, one small anthology, and three other titles.*					
RIGBY LITERACY					
RIGBY FOCUS					
RIGBY LIGHTHOUSE					
WRIGHT GROUP *Storybox, Sunshine, and Foundations Sets.*					
SUNDANCE *Alpha Kids, Little Red, and Blue and Green Readers.*					
ROSEN READERS *Great photographs, with emphasis on content.*					
SEEDLING *Small company. Written by ex-Reading Recovery teachers.*					
MODERN CURRICULUM PRESS *More controlled vocabulary than most.*					
BENCHMARK *Early Connections set. Good low-level stories.*					
DOMINIE *All sets.*					
MONDO *Leveled books that come in a variety sizes and formats. Features renowned authors.*					
PACIFIC LEARNING *Some older Richard Owens titles that teachers like.*					
NATIONAL GEOGRAPHIC *Leveled, wonderful content, excellent pictures. Different sets for each grade level.*					
KAEDEN BOOKS					
BEBOP BOOKS *Multicultural, leveled books.*					

Planning Effective Read-Alouds

TARGET

Elementary ✓   Middle School/High School ✓

Read-alouds have long been a staple in primary classrooms. The image of a teacher reading aloud with a picture book turned toward a group of young children seated on a rug is iconic. When primary teachers were asked why they did read-alouds, many said they wanted children to enjoy literature or that the read-aloud introduced or reinforced a seasonal theme, such as Thanksgiving or spring. Sometimes, primary teachers told literacy coaches that read-alouds were a great way to calm down students after recess or lunch.

Today, however, read-alouds are gaining stature across all grade levels and for multiple purposes. Lester L. Laminack and Reba M. Wadsworth (2006) suggest that teachers can choose to read aloud to all K–12 students to build community, teach poetry, provide mentor texts for writing workshops, make important connections to content curriculum, and provide entrance to the vocabulary and music of language.

This new prominence in read-alouds adds to the literacy coach's duties. Coaches are responsible for choosing appropriate books, setting purposes, inspiring student engagement, stocking classroom and school libraries, and knowing the literature. You can use the Read-Aloud Checklist and Planning Guide to provide teachers with a structure for using read-alouds in their lessons.

Reference for further learning

Laminack, L. L., & Wadsworth, R. M. (2006). *Learning under the influence of language and literature: Making the most of read-alouds across the day.* Portsmouth, NH: Heinemann.

GOALS

- To improve the quality, quantity, and purpose of read-aloud sessions.
- To help provide structure for the teacher.
- To begin maintaining plans for reading the same book to future classes.

IMPLEMENTATION

1. Make the planning guide available to teachers who expressed an interest in improving their read-aloud sessions. It might also be used as part of a coaching cycle (see "The Coaching Cycle" on page 54).

2. It may be helpful to develop a coaching contract (see "Coaching by Contract" on page 58) that clarifies the roles of the coach and teacher and the time line for providing coaching support.

3. Prompt the teacher to identify a purpose for planning this read-aloud (e.g., mentor text for writing, vocabulary development, building community, ending the day, teaching poetry, connecting to content curriculum, or allowing students reading below grade level to access textbook content).

4. Collaborate with the teacher to select an appropriate book that fulfills the purpose of the read-aloud.

5. Read through the book together, plan an introduction to the book, and identify words for explicit vocabulary instruction and stopping points for thinking aloud and comprehension.

6. Work with the teacher to fill out the Read-Aloud Checklist and Planning Guide.

7. After the read aloud, ask the teacher to use the back of the form to write comments, student responses, and ideas for adjusting instruction the next time they use the book.

8. You can copy and share completed forms at grade-level meetings.

REFLECTION, EVALUATION, AND PLANNING

1. How will you know whether this form promoted more thoughtful selections of titles for read-alouds? Is there anything you need to add to the form to make it more helpful to teachers?

2. How are students responding to the read-alouds?

3. Which teachers might be willing to share their work with this particular read-aloud at a grade-level meeting? Is there another way to share the work of teachers, such as by videotaping?

4. Are there adequate books available for multiple read-alouds in a day? If not, how can you add additional titles or copies to the teachers' collections?

5. Plan a book club (see "Forming a Teacher Book Club" on page 196) or study group (see "Planning a Teachers' Study Group" on page 192) around read-aloud methods or the benefits of read-alouds and advertise the opportunity to staff.

Read-Aloud Checklist and Planning Guide

Title _____

Author _____

Check those items that relate to this read-aloud.

- ☐ I have a clear purpose and plan for choosing this book.
- ☐ This book is at my students' level of understanding but above their instructional reading level.
- ☐ This book represents a new genre for this week.
- ☐ I have identified 2–3 words for further vocabulary instruction.
- ☐ I have designated 2–3 stopping points for discussion and thinking aloud.
- ☐ I have other books in my classroom library by this author.
- ☐ I have other books on this topic in my classroom library.
- ☐ I am using this book to extend my students' knowledge in content area topics.
- ☐ I can use this book as a mentor text for writing.
- ☐ This book is fiction but I can pair it with expository (or narrative) text or a poem.
- ☐ I have a plan to make this book available to my students after the read-aloud.

Words for vocabulary instruction:

Stopping points for thinking aloud and discussion:

PART 2

Guiding a Small-Group Reading Lesson

TARGET
Elementary ✓   Middle School/High School __

"Can you help me with my guided-reading groups?" That may be one of the most frequent requests a literacy coach hears. The following Guided Reading Planning Sheet is designed to support the literacy coach's efforts to make the teacher's plan for guided-reading groups more effective and more efficient.

One of the literacy coach's first tasks is to help teachers identify the current reading level of their students using running records (see "Taking a Running Record" on page 75) or by another means. The teacher can then group students who read at approximately the same level (see "Appropriately Grouping Students" on page 81).

The next step is to select a suitable text, and here the literacy coach can help the teacher choose a book that is not only at the right level, but that also matches the needs of the group. For instance, a group of students reading at level C who are struggling with phonics may need a book with strong illustrations to reinforce their reading. For a group reading at level C with stronger phonics skills, illustrations may not be as important. Literacy coaches can help teachers learn how to present the book to the small group.

The Guided Reading Planning Sheet can provide teachers with a helpful structure for planning an introduction the book or to reinforce the strategies that the groups' running records suggest they need. The plan might include stopping points to check comprehension, what vocabulary the teacher might need to discuss, and the kinds of closings the teacher might use.

If you find that teachers are struggling with guided reading, see "Troubleshooting for a Small-Group Reading Lesson" on page 128 to read about support strategies.

GOALS

- To support the literacy coach's work with teachers interested in moving to small-group reading instruction—as opposed to whole-group instruction in which all students read the same book.
- To help teachers better understand the power of careful preparation before introducing a new book.
- To help teachers plan a brief, thoughtful lesson plan to prepare students to read and comprehend a new text during a small-group or guided-reading lesson.
- To build a collection of brief, thoughtful lesson plans that teachers can share with each other and use with future groups reading the same books.

IMPLEMENTATION

1. Help teachers assess students' running records to determine what level of book most closely matches their current reading achievement.
2. Support the teacher in grouping students who would benefit from reading the same level book. After assigning them to a group and reading one or two books together, the teacher can confirm whether the grouping is right.
3. Collaborate with the teacher to study available titles for the group's reading level.
4. Help the teacher select a text, considering the challenges the book may present given the needs of the group who will read it.
5. Using the Guided Reading Planning Sheet, collaborate with the teacher to develop a guided-reading lesson.
6. Ask the teacher to refer to the plan during the guided-reading lesson, making notes where needed, to record the students' response to the book and the plan.
7. Meet with the teacher after implementing the plan to reflect on its effectiveness and where you can revise the plan.
8. Ask the teacher to retain a copy of the plan (or revised plan), along with a copy of the book, to use with future groups. Remind the teacher to review the plan prior to using it with the next group to assure that it matches their needs.

REFLECTION, EVALUATION, AND PLANNING

1. If possible, secure funds to purchase binders in which teachers can store plans.
2. How can teachers share guided-reading plans with each other?

3. Whenever possible, observe teachers as they lead their guided-reading lessons to determine where they may need to revise their planning.

4. Survey teaches to find out whether they find the planning sheet helpful. Edit the planning sheet where appropriate.

5. At grade-level meetings, encourage teachers to discuss how they can reflect on their progress with guided reading and what they might have done differently to avoid unexpected challenges.

6. If teachers struggle with aspects of guided reading—for example, finding the most effective stopping points for students—what professional development can you provide?

Guided Reading Planning Sheet

Title _____

Author _____ Book Level _____

Strategies to emphasize (connections, visualization, DR-TA, DWL, purpose for reading, etc.):

Vocabulary to be introduced:

Challenges to be noted before students read:

Stopping points for discussion during reading:

Possibilities for response:

Source: Adapted with permission from the work of Evelyn Acevedo-Nolfi, literacy coach at Avondale School, Chicago, Ill.

Troubleshooting for a Small-Group Reading Lesson

TARGET
Elementary ✓   Middle School/High School __

For guided reading to be effective, the literacy coach must support teachers at the right stage and group teachers who have the same needs. The Guided-Reading Self-Assessment can help coaches gather information about the needs of individual teachers and group them for support.

Guided reading is an instructional strategy in which teachers support each reader's development of effective strategies for processing new text at increasing levels of difficulty (Pinnell & Fountas, 1996). First, teachers assess students to determine their instructional reading levels (see "Taking a Running Record" on page 75). Then they form groups of four to six children with similar instructional needs (see "Appropriately Grouping Students" on page 81) and conduct daily guided-reading lessons using carefully level books (see "Guiding a Small-Group Reading Lesson" on page 124).

The lesson begins with a supportive introduction to the book. Afterward, the teacher monitors students as they read and offers support as needed. Based on the teacher's observation of that group of students' reading, the teacher follows up with a lesson. While the teacher is working with one small group of readers, the other students are working on independent literacy activities.

Implementing a successful guided-reading program on a daily basis requires the teacher to have a high level of knowledge and skill. It can be significantly more demanding than using a core reading textbook. The literacy coach can be a valuable resource for teachers, helping them successfully implement this kind of small-group reading instruction. The Guided-Reading Self-Assessment can help teachers pinpoint a starting place so that the literacy coach can fine-tune guided reading. Literacy coaches can also use the self-assessment as a framework to plan a coaching cycle (see "The Coaching Cycle" on page 54).

Reference for further learning

Pinnell, G. S., & Fountas, I. (1996). *Guided reading: Good first teaching for all children.* Portsmouth, NH: Heinemann.

GOALS

- To support teachers in identifying challenges in implementing guided reading.
- To collaborate with teachers to develop a plan to fine-tune their guided-reading instruction.

IMPLEMENTATION

1. Give the Guided-Reading Self-Assessment to a teacher who solicits your support with guided reading, and ask the teacher to complete the form.
2. Schedule a conference to discuss the teacher's self-assessment.
3. Observe the teacher in class during a guided-reading lesson and take notes. Share what you have written with the teacher.
4. Meet with the teacher to develop an action plan that includes learning goals for students. Consider creating a coaching contract (see "Coaching by Contract" on page 58) to clarify goals and roles. Begin the action plan with aspects that the teacher can quickly adjust with little difficulty, then move to more challenging goals. Make a time line to work on quick wins and longer-term objectives.
5. Systematically work through the list and continue to visit the classroom periodically during guided-reading lessons to assess progress and guide the teacher to the reading goals you outlined.

REFLECTION, EVALUATION, AND PLANNING

1. In what ways do the original self-assessment and additional updates continue to reflect a reasonable state of readiness?
2. In what areas do you need to remind the teacher about certain aspects of guided-reading lessons (e.g. taking a running record or doing a book introduction)?
3. What other colleagues might like to join a book club (see "Forming a Teacher Book Club" on page 196) about one or more facet of guided reading? This could promote sharing between teachers who are working on the same issue.
4. Have you helped teachers set up a study group (see "Planning a Teachers' Study Group" on page 192) about guided reading? If not, what other classroom might a teacher visit to watch a colleague conduct a guided-reading lesson?

5. Would this teacher benefit from a coaching cycle?

6. As you work with the teacher to troubleshoot challenging aspects of guided reading, is there an effective way to share this work with others? Would sharing at a grade-level meeting (see "Organizing Grade-Level and Department Meetings" on page 188) be appropriate? Or perhaps collecting videotapes of the teacher's progress over time?

7. Identify any physical conditions, such as the proximity of literacy centers or furniture configuration, that the teacher can alter to improve guided-reading lessons.

Guided-Reading Self-Assessment

Identify the degree to which you have established each component of guided reading.

	Firmly Established	Partially Established	Initiated	Not Initiated Yet
Initial assessment *Completed assessments for all students and have a reading level for each.*				
Leveled book library *Sufficient number of books to provide instruction for all students at their instructional level for the school year.*				
Groups *Formation of a manageable number of groups; each group has an appropriate number of students for optimal instruction.*				
Schedule *Manageable schedule of meeting with each group an adequate number of times per week; meeting with the neediest group daily.*				
Matching books to students *Books selected for lessons are at my students' instructional level.*				
Instruction *Lessons included supportive introductions, scaffolding, and monitoring as needed during reading and targeted follow-up minilessons based on observation of student reading.*				
Running records *A routine of administering a running record to one student in each group and using the information to make instructional decisions.*				
Dynamic grouping *A routine of using running records and observations to reform groups in order to fine-tune instruction.*				
Management *A routine of engaging students in meaningful, independent literacy activities while I work with small groups.*				
Independent practice *Students have the opportunity to reread books during guided-reading lessons and read other books at their independent and instructional levels to practice strategies taught during guided-reading lessons.*				

PART 2

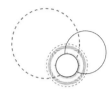

Planning for Shared Reading

TARGET

Elementary ✔   Middle School/High School ___

Shared reading was developed to simulate the bedtime story in the classroom. An especially valuable whole-group literacy technique, it simultaneously enables students who already read to read the text conventionally and students just learning to read to be assisted by the teacher.

During shared reading, teachers engage students in reading an enlarged text that contains supportive features, usually including rhyme, rhythm, and repetition, for children just learning how to read. Teachers read the same enlarged book repeatedly over a period of up to five days. The rhyme, rhythm, and repetition enable the students to more easily memorize the text. While reading, the teachers track the text with a pointer or their finger to help students make the connection between the spoken word and the print on the page.

With each reading, the students' ability to read the text accurately along with the teacher increases. After the initial reading of the text, teachers use the book to teach beginning reading skills, such as word recognition, phonics, phonemic awareness, and text conventions. After several rereadings, teachers may also make standard-size copies of the texts for the students to read on their own. The literacy coach might suggest that teachers display copies of the text in the room and make the book available to groups of children who want to reread it together. A teacher may also put copies of the standard-size text with an audio recording in a Listening Center.

The literacy coach's support can ensure the success of shared reading. You can maintain a collection of appropriate texts for shared reading in the literacy resource room or closet (see "Organizing a Literacy Closet" on page 208). You can also secure enlarged texts related to the themes and content area topics taught in grades K–2. During grade-level meetings (see "Organizing Grade-Level and Department Meetings" on page 188), the coach can moderate lesson planning about specific enlarged-text books, encouraging teachers to make connections to their school's grade-level literacy curriculum topics.

You can use the Shared Reading Planning Sheet with grade-level groups of teachers or with a single teacher who is new to the primary grades. The steps below are for a grade-level group, but you can easily adapt them to work effectively with a teacher one-on-one.

Reference for further learning

Holdaway, D. (1979). *Foundations of literacy.* New York: Scholastic.

GOALS

- To provide a rich way to teach reading in the context of real text.
- To specifically address the beginning needs of young readers (e.g., print to text match, phonics, concept of word, conventions, and rhyme).
- To provide literacy instruction and, at the same time, expose children to children's literature, especially in the areas of poetry, nursery rhymes, and genres considered important for young readers.
- To provide a safe way for teachers to address the needs of all children in a whole-group setting.
- To provide a small-group intervention for children struggling to acquire beginning literacy skills.

IMPLEMENTATION

1. Plan a shared reading lesson plan session for an upcoming grade-level meeting in grades K–2.
2. Give each teacher a copy of the planning sheet.
3. Model a shared-reading lesson. While you read aloud and display the big book or other enlarged text, examine the book for teaching possibilities in phonemic awareness, phonics, sight words, comprehension, vocabulary, and print conventions. Encourage teachers to look for ways to use the book with their particular students.
4. Discuss possible extension activities and text innovations.
5. Ask for a volunteer to try out the lesson and arrange for other teachers to visit the classroom to watch.
6. Retain a copy of the plan for future reference.

ASCD 133

REFLECTION, EVALUATION, AND PLANNING

1. If working with a small group of teachers, what was the level of involvement of each teacher? If some were less involved, how can you remedy that for the next group?

2. How would you rate the lesson's ability to actively engage students?

3. After working with a teacher or group, what additional professional development do they still need? If a study group (see "Planning a Teachers' Study Group" on page 192) or coaching cycle (see "The Coaching Cycle" on page 54) might be helpful, how will you approach teachers to initiate one or both?

4. How will you determine whether all shared reading books are appropriate? Consider size of text, length, content, and so forth.

5. What is your financial plan to ensure that all primary classrooms have sufficient materials for daily shared reading lessons? You may need to plan for multiple-year purchasing.

Shared Reading Planning Sheet

Title _____

Author _____

Phonemic Awareness Concepts
Phonics Concepts
Sight Words to be Taught
Words for Vocabulary Instruction
Print Conventions to be Taught
Comprehension Concepts
Extension Activities
Innovation

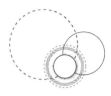

Introducing Student Book Clubs

TARGET
Elementary ✔   Middle School/High School ✔

Book clubs can be an exciting alternative setting for literacy instruction. They allow teachers to differentiate instruction according to interest and motivate students to read by letting them choose the topic.

The teacher selects a group of books that are of varying levels and interests but that have a common genre or theme. Students preview the books or listen to book talks and then choose their top three. Students read and write independently but come together for discussions with others who chose the same book. The teacher can move about the room, joining groups and guiding students to think about the text.

Depending on the needs of the group, the teacher can introduce particular topics, such as the components and structure of biographies, through minilessons prior to reading. This gives students other features to focus on as they read. Even for those students who easily enter into discussions, teachers can ask them to focus on an element as a way to practice literacy strategies and skills.

Students generally keep logs to document their thinking as they read, and these logs can be the foundation for their discussions. For instance, as they read they note literary elements such as author's craft or intriguing and challenging words; or interpret and analyze what they read; or think about point of view, title explanation, or connections to other texts.

Literacy coaches can help teachers plan and evaluate a book club by providing them with the following Book Club Plan worksheet.

References for further learning

Blachowicz, C., & Ogle, D. (2001). *Reading comprehension: Strategies for independent learners*. New York: Guilford Press.

McMahon, S. I., Raphael, T. E., Goatley, V. J., & Pardo, L. S. (Eds.). (1997). *The book club connection: Literacy learning and classroom talk*. New York: Teachers College Press.

GOALS

- To help students take more active roles in reading and talking about books.
- To motivate students to read by allowing them to choose the books and discussion topics.
- To prompt teachers to think about the content of their classroom libraries.

IMPLEMENTATION

1. Develop a coaching plan for implementing student book clubs that includes a time line and clearly delineated roles for both the teacher and the coach. Using a contract (see "Coaching by Contract" on page 58) may be helpful.

2. Identify one or more student learning goals, such as increased student discussion around books or evidence of increased interest in reading.

3. Consider how to evaluate whether book clubs are meeting the teacher's learning goal for students. For example, if increased student discussion is a goal, how will the teacher know that happens?

4. Include a plan to let students see and hear a live book club discussion. You may try a Fishbowl: In this modeling tool, students watch and listen while the teacher and a group of colleagues have a book discussion. Sometimes students are comfortable modeling for the class.

5. Determine whether the teacher wants to form a study group (see "Planning a Teachers' Study Group" on page 192) with colleagues who are also interested in student book clubs.

6. Determine how to share the teacher's book club efforts with other staff. Would this best happen during visitations, grade-level meetings, or staff meetings?

REFLECTION, EVALUATION, AND PLANNING

1. How did students respond to book clubs?
2. What was the nature and depth of student discussions?
3. What kind of modeling or support does the teacher still need?
4. How are students progressing with the teacher's learning goal?
5. Is the teacher's method of evaluating students' progress appropriate?
6. What additional book titles are needed for future book clubs?
7. Which book clubs topics would the teacher like to study with a group of colleagues?
8. Work with the teacher to develop a plan to share book club outcomes with colleagues. Consider allowing visitors to observe, sharing outcomes at grade-level or staff meetings, or reporting to the school literacy team (see "Creating a School Literacy Team" on page 181).

Book Club Plan

Title _____

Author _____

Group Members:

1. _____   5. _____

2. _____   6. _____

3. _____   7. _____

4. _____   8. _____

Student Learning Goals:

1.

2.

Evaluation:

Notes:

Introducing and Supporting Read and Relax (R&R)

TARGET
Elementary ✓   Middle School/High School ✓

Adults frequently read a book as a way to relax. Read and Relax (R&R) is a daily classroom reading routine that tries to duplicate that experience for students. The teacher sets aside 20–30 minutes per day for students to read independently in texts at their print reading level, which is usually considered the level at which they can read with fluency, smoothness, and 98–99 percent accuracy. The goal is to have students enjoy reading texts that are not chosen to teach reading but to provide a relaxing and pleasing experience.

Unlike some forms of independent reading, such as sustained silent reading, R&R requires the teacher to take an active role, checking that students have chosen books at the proper level. To model fluency for the class, on the first day the teacher can read from a relaxing book and then from a challenging book, such as a medical book or technical manual. The teacher may have to artificially slow down during the difficult text and should avoid referring to the words as "easy" or "hard".

Each day students pick their books, go to their seats or to R&R areas, and begin reading silently (very young readers may still read orally). The teacher moves around the room, quietly asking to hear a bit of each book. This brief listening helps the teacher confirm that students have picked appropriate books. If they have, the teacher can offer a brief comment, such as, "You like mystery novels, don't you?" Or, "Share that book with Mary. I think she'd like it." If the student picks a book that is too challenging, the teacher can either help pick a different one or negotiate, asking that the next book be more relaxing for them. The interaction with each student can be less than one minute.

In the case of very young and emergent readers, R&R books will not be rich text, so it is important for teachers to continue to read aloud so that students can practice comprehending richer, more complex texts. As teachers and students become used to the routine, some teachers allow 2–3 minutes for students to share their book with a partner before ending R&R.

ASCD □ 139

Note taking is entirely optional, but some teachers do like to keep track of several indicators when they are monitoring R&R: whether students are able to pick out books that are at their personal reading level, whether they have the stamina to read consistently for 20–30 minutes at a time, and whether they seem to enjoy—or even look forward to or request additional time for—R&R on a daily basis. To help guide teachers' reflection of students' responses to R&R, the literacy coach can provide teachers with the following Teacher Notes: Response to Read and Relax sheet.

References for further learning

Johns, G., & Berglund, R. (2005). *Fluency: Strategies and assessments* (2nd ed.). Dubuque, IA: Kendall/ Hunt Publishing.

Maro, N. (2001). Reading to improve fluency. *Illinois Reading Council Journal, 29*(3), 10–18.

Rasinski, R., Blachowicz, C., & Lems, K. (2006). *Fluency instruction: Research-based best practices.* New York: Guilford Press.

GOALS

- To introduce a structure that helps students learn to select books that will improve their fluency, develop their own reading interests, and instill a habit and love of reading.
- To provide a format for teachers to hear students read one-on-one.
- To help teachers understand how independent-level text reading can improve student fluency and reading enjoyment.
- To help teachers become more familiar with and think deeply about the selection of books in their classroom libraries.

IMPLEMENTATION

1. Work with the teacher to design a plan that outlines both the teacher's and the literacy coach's roles and the time line for implementing R&R together. Consider using a coaching contract (see "Coaching by Contract" on page 58).
2. Use the teacher's knowledge, observations of students, and student data to identify one or more student learning goals, such as increasing the desire to read or improving reading rate.
3. Revise the current classroom schedule to accommodate R&R.
4. Decide how to measure the influence of R&R on student learning. If fluency is a goal, one option would be a one-minute classroom fluency snapshot (see "Taking a Fluency Snapshot" on page 96). If increased interest is a goal, a reading inventory survey may be a good choice.

5. Study the classroom library (see "Analyzing Classroom Libraries" on page 204) to see how it will support R&R. You may suggest a multiyear plan to increase appropriate texts. For the short term, you can check out books from many public libraries in bulk on teacher loans.

6. Depending on the roles outlined in the teacher-coach action plan, you may model soliciting student reading during R&R, showing the kind of responses to students that are not evaluative, and model how to negotiate with students to select books at their own reading level.

REFLECTION, EVALUATION, AND PLANNING

1. What information does the teacher gather from listening to students read aloud during R&R each day? Does it provide insights into student fluency, student interests, or their ability to share thoughts?

2. How are students responding to R&R? Are they moving toward the teacher's learning goals for them?

3. Which proficient readers might respond to encouragement to expand their reading to other genres?

4. Which students are not responding positively to the routine of R&R? Can you suggest changes to make it a more productive experience for them? Would finding alternative titles or adding more titles at a particular level help?

5. Based on teacher response and student outcomes, what are the topics teachers might want to study with a group of colleagues (see "Planning a Teachers' Study Group" on page 192)?

6. How might teachers share their work with colleagues? Can you set up a grade-level meeting (see "Organizing Grade-Level and Department Meetings" on page 188), arrange to have the classroom videotaped during R&R, or ask a teacher to present at a conference?

PART 2

Teacher Notes: Response to Read and Relax

Date _____

Key: 1 = Little or no resources
     2 = Developing
     3 = Solid

Student Name	Selects Books at Independent Level	Shows Stamina for Entire R&R Period	Enjoys Reading During R&R	Additional Comments

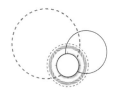

Using the Language Experience Approach (LEA)

TARGET
Elementary ✓   Middle School/High School __

When students create a text, they are also forming an enduring understanding of language. In the language experience approach (LEA), early readers dictate a story in their own language about a shared experience, and the teacher records their ideas on chart paper. These activities with both spoken and written words provide a rich context for students to make the connection between them and to learn the beginning literacy skills the teacher is focusing on, such as the concept of word, beginning sounds, and certain letter formations.

The shared experience for an LEA might be a field trip, observing the first snowfall of the year, a fire drill, or a classroom celebration. In this technique, the teacher gathers the students to elicit their responses to the event, sometimes selecting a theme around which to structure the dictation. For instance, "What Snow Looks Like During the First Snowfall." Then students talk with a partner and the teacher can ask for volunteers to share with the whole group. This gives every child a chance to use the language of the topic and then listen to others talk before beginning to write.

As students offer their beginning dictation, the teacher writes their sentences on chart paper large enough for all children to read. For children beginning kindergarten, the teacher will only take a short dictation of two to four sentences. As the year goes on, the same class can produce longer LEAs. The teacher uses instructional language to guide the sequence and accuracy of the story, encouraging complete sentences, saying the words aloud as they are written, repeating sentences to help generate the next sentence, and asking students to reread.

A completed LEA may look like this: It started snowing when we were in school. There were big snowflakes. We want to go out to recess now. We want to play in the snow!

When the dictation is finished, the chart story can become a permanent reading opportunity for many months to follow. The teacher can reread it over many days and tape it to the classroom wall.

After the teacher has used an LEA over a period of weeks, the literacy coach can introduce the Record of Student Learning During LEA as a way for the teacher to document some of the students' reading behaviors as they dictate, reread, and work with the text.

References for further learning

Tierney, R. J., Readance, J. E., & Dishner, E. K. (1990). *Reading strategies and practices: A compendium.* Boston: Allyn & Bacon.

Van Allen, R. (1976). *Language experience in communication.* Boston: Houghton Mifflin.

GOALS

- To use the language, experiences, and thoughts of children to teach them how to read.
- To help teachers see and understand the connection between oral and written language through the eyes of instruction.
- To highlight the way children can use their own language to help them remember how to read beginning texts.
- To provide a collection of readable text that teachers can use with their youngest readers.
- To emphasize the importance of using a variety of texts to teach reading.
- To provide a planning sheet that will help teachers take next steps after an LEA dictation.

IMPLEMENTATION

1. Brainstorm with the teacher to choose an appropriate experience on which to base a language experience text.
2. Talk about the key beginning literacy skills that the teacher believes children should know at this point in the school year. Identify up to three skills—for example, a simple sight word, a particular letter sound, or the spaces between words—that might be appropriate to emphasize during the dictation process.
3. Present some possible sentences that students might dictate and see how the teacher might handle those words or letters on the first reading or on subsequent readings later in the week.
4. Work with the teacher to help schedule a time for this instructional strategy, a time that can be repeated during different days of the week.
5. Consider developing a contract (see "Coaching by Contract" on page 58) that details what the teacher hopes students will learn, a time line for learning, and roles that both you and the teacher will fill.

6. Set a time to debrief about how the first LEA went and what future support you might offer.

7. Introduce the teacher to the Record of Student Learning During LEA.

REFLECTION, EVALUATION, AND PLANNING

1. How would you describe teachers' comfort level with planning and implementing LEAs in the classroom?

2. What particular aspects of beginning literacy do teachers need to know or have more information about? How could you initiate a study group (see "Planning a Teachers' Study Group" on page 192) or book club (see "Forming a Teacher Book Club" on page 196) about this topic?

3. If you are working with a teacher new to the grade level, is there an experienced teacher who might be willing to be observed? If that is not possible, how can you position yourself to provide modeling for the new teacher?

Record of Student Learning During LEA

Week of: _____

Name	Accurate Voice/ Print Match	Automatic Word ID	Echo Reading Support	Word ID By Tracking	No Word ID	Letter/Sound Recognition

Source: Adapted with permission from the work of Barbara Kaufman, project facilitator at National-Louis University in Skokie, Ill.

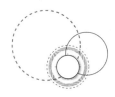

Implementing Poem of the Week

TARGET
Elementary ✓   Middle School/High School ___

Poem of the Week is a strategy that combines reading instruction with children's poetry in ways that allow students to enjoy both. Repeated choral readings of the same poem daily over a five-day period gives students a chance to read, learn about, and enjoy the poem more deeply. Poem of the Week also gives teachers an opportunity to teach or reinforce a carefully planned variety of literacy skills.

First, the teacher selects a poem and writes it on chart paper, displaying it prominently in the classroom. Led by the teacher, students read the poem aloud in unison every day for five days. Before, during, and after the readings, the poem becomes a context for teaching a love of poetry, vocabulary, phonics, comprehension, and more. The repeated readings also help improve students' fluency.

If the teacher sets up related literacy centers, students can get additional practice reading and manipulating the poems. The centers can invite students to illustrate single lines from the poem, assemble pages to create a class book, or make their own copy on standard-size paper to retain in their poetry notebooks. At the end of the school year, students can take home a notebook of 40 poems that they know, love, and can read.

To save time, teachers are often tempted to purchase ready-made Poem of the Week lessons. However, if the poems in the kits are written for instructional purposes, they may not match the quality of the poems written by poets for the joy of reading. The literacy coach is paramount in building a collection of high-quality poetry and supporting teachers in implementing the Poem of the Week strategy.

You can collaborate with the teacher to select poems, design lessons, and implement a clear plan to turn over responsibility to the teacher over time. To make sure the teacher is taking advantage of all aspects of the strategy, you can work with them to complete the Poem of the Week Planning Sheet. Eventually teachers can use the sheet on their own.

GOALS

- To provide additional methods to teach literacy skills such as vocabulary, phonics, and comprehension.
- To expose students to the joys of reading and listening to poetry.
- To build a sense of community that shared reading can bring to a classroom.

IMPLEMENTATION

1. Working closely with the teacher, design a plan that outlines both the teacher's and the coach's roles and the time line for implementation. Using a contract (see "Coaching by Contract" on page 58) here may be helpful.
2. Use the teacher's knowledge, observations of students, and student data to identify one or more learning goals.
3. Consider how you will know if the teacher's goals are being met through Poem of the Week—what will students have to demonstrate and where will they show it?
4. Collaborate with the teacher to select a poem that meets the goals and is appropriate for the students' grade level and interests.
5. Use the Poem of the Week Planning Sheet to outline five days of minilessons related to the goals. Lessons should take approximately five minutes of class time.
6. Plan with the teacher how to use the poem to highlight and implement the minilesson.
7. Write the poem on chart paper.
8. Schedule the first Poem of the Week. The teacher may want to do it alone and then share outcomes or may want you to observe or coteach. This should all be detailed in the contract or plan.
9. Make a copy of the first poem on standard-size paper, and attach the planning sheet for future use of the same poem.

REFLECTION, EVALUATION, AND PLANNING

1. Reflect with the teacher about how students responded to the first poem. Did they retain their enthusiasm for the poem over the entire five days? If not, why?
2. Reflect on the length of the session, the focus of skills emphasized, and how engaging the poem was for students.
3. Prompt the teacher to reflect on the relationship between the poem and the skills taught. Are the skills a natural extension of the poem and not artificial?

4. Did the teacher become more comfortable with selecting and planning lessons after the first week?

5. Based on outcomes with students, what topics might the teacher want to study with a group of colleagues (see "Planning a Teachers' Study Group" on page 192)?

6. Would other teachers be interested in trying the Poem of the Week strategy? Can you arrange for the original teacher to share work with colleagues?

Poem of the Week Planning Sheet

Poem Title _____

Author and Reference _____

_____

Recommended Grade Level _____

Minilessons

Phonics Concepts
Vocabulary
Comprehension Strategies
Text Connections
_____
_____

Comments:

Introducing Knowledge Rating

TARGET
Elementary ✔   Middle School/High School ✔

Knowledge Rating is a vocabulary strategy designed to help students think about how well they understand a key set of words needed to make sense of an assigned text. Before reading, they are asked to sort a list of words from the text into one of three categories:

- Can Define the Word
- Know Something About the Word
- Don't Know This Word

The goal is to help students begin to understand what the text demands and where they need to concentrate their efforts. The activity can provide the same kind of window for teachers to consider where to focus their instruction.

The teacher first reads the text and selects words key to understanding. Teacher's guides may provide these lists, but teachers may sometimes select alternative words based on what they know about their students.

The teacher then customizes the Knowledge Rating Sheet with the words and distributes it to students. In some cases, teachers post the words on the board and ask students to draw their own graphic organizer on paper or in a journal.

Students are asked to predict what the words might mean before they start reading. As students encounter the words in the text, they may need to use a dictionary or glossary and reread the section containing that word. If the context or text explains the meaning of the word, no further work may be necessary.

The literacy coach can provide teachers with a form that they can customize for each text. A standardized form can help students know what to expect during the activity and help teachers interpret the results. Teachers can adapt the activity and even the graphic to best suit their needs.

Reference for further learning

Blachowicz, C., & Fisher, P. J. (2002). *Teaching vocabulary in all classrooms.* Upper Saddle River, NJ: Prentice Hall.

GOALS

- To alert students and teachers to the vocabulary demands of a text before students begin to read it.
- To encourage teacher understanding about the importance of vocabulary instruction.
- To show teachers that word knowledge develops along a continuum.
- To provide a user-friendly graphic organizer that helps both teachers and students know where to concentrate their efforts.

IMPLEMENTATION

1. In cooperation with the teacher, design a plan that outlines the teacher's and the coach's roles and the time line to independently using the knowledge rating strategy and graphic organizer. Using a contract (see "Coaching by Contract" on page 58) may be helpful.
2. Select a content area that currently presents a vocabulary challenge to students, and choose a reasonable learning goal for students.
3. Discuss how the teacher will know if and when students reach the goal. For example, will students take some type of vocabulary assessment? Or will the teacher look for a change in the level of discussion after reading?
4. Select a set of words that seem key to understanding the next section of text. Use the teacher's guide or the teacher's own choice of vocabulary.
5. Plan the type of support most helpful to the teacher, be it modeling, observation and feedback, or collecting resources.

REFLECTION, EVALUATION, AND PLANNING

1. How did teachers evaluate the effect of their vocabulary efforts? How did the assessment increase their understanding of what students had learned?
2. Reflect on the quality and quantity of the vocabulary teachers identified. Was it appropriate? How can you work with the teacher to improve the selection in future readings?
3. If the teachers are willing, how might they share the work they are doing on vocabulary? With teacher permission, consider videotaping a lesson and sharing it at a whole-school staff development meeting or making it available to teachers to view on their own.

4. Is there a group of teachers who might want dig deeper into vocabulary with a study group (see "Planning a Teachers' Study Group" on page 192)?

5. How will you know when to the teacher is ready to use the strategy without your support? What checks will you have in place to make sure the teacher sustains the activity in appropriate places over time?

Knowledge Rating Sheet

Name _____

Subject _____ Text _____

Date _____

Word	Can Define the Word	Know Something About the Word	Don't Know This Word

Introducing the Predict-O-Gram

TARGET
Elementary ✓   Middle School/High School ✓

Predict-O-Gram is a prereading strategy for narrative text that emphasizes story structure, vocabulary, and the power of predictions. With these elements in mind, students can focus on them as they read. The strategy introduces stories to students in a way that will increase their ability to understand what they will read and build on their capacity to use story elements to increase comprehension.

The literacy coach can supply teachers with a standardized Predict-O-Gram graphic that they can distribute to the class. The Predict-O-Gram chart provides students with a structure to match story words to predetermined categories:

- Words about where/when the story takes place
- Words about the characters in the story
- Words about the actions in the story
- Words about the story's resolution
- Words that describe the problem
- Other things

Teachers can let students work individually or in partners. After categorizing the words on the graphic, students make a prediction about the story and construct a question about some aspect of the story. Actively engaged in the task, students are drawn into the reading to follow.

It's important for students to have an opportunity to share their predictions with each other, either in small groups or with a partner, before they begin reading. Teachers can ask them to explain how and why they categorized the words as they did and what about the words led them to their prediction and question.

During a post-reading discussion, the teacher can ask students to compare their predictions to what the author actually wrote and summarize their understanding of the story.

Reference for further learning

Blachowicz, C., & Fisher, P. J. (2002). *Teaching vocabulary in all classrooms.* Upper Saddle River, NJ: Prentice Hall.

GOALS

- To give students a graphic organizer based on story structure and vocabulary that provides a chance for them to actively make predictions.
- To increase teacher understanding of the importance of story structure, vocabulary, and prediction in increasing student comprehension.
- To help teachers identify stories with clearly delineated story elements to support instruction.

IMPLEMENTATION

1. In cooperation with the teacher, design a plan that outlines both the teacher's and the coach's roles and the time line for the teacher independently using the Predict-O-Gram organizer. Using a contract (see "Coaching by Contract" on page 58) may be helpful.
2. Use the teacher's knowledge, observations of students, and student data to identify one or more student learning goals that the Predict-O-Gram activity can support. For example, if students have been struggling to understand setting, the learning goal could be a certain percentage of students able to competently place appropriate words in the "setting" cell.
3. Work with the teacher to plan minilessons about story elements related to the graphic organizer and, in particular, the established learning goal.

REFLECTION, EVALUATION, AND PLANNING

1. How did students respond to the Predict-O-Gram chart?
2. In what ways did the teacher's method of evaluating the learning goal match the goal itself?
3. Work with the teacher to reflect on student participation to decide which story elements seem solid and which remain a challenge. What minilessons could address the problem areas?
4. Is there evidence that the Predict-O-Gram helped students discuss story elements or better understand them?
5. Are there other teachers who might want to join a study group (see "Planning a Teachers' Study Group" on page 192) about how to enhance instruction on any of the story elements?
6. Would the teacher be willing to share experiences with the Predict-O-Gram with other colleagues? Could you arrange to have the teacher's classroom available for visitors to observe or could you share student work at grade-level meetings?

Predict-O-Gram

Name(s) _____

Book Title _____

Words about where/when the story takes place:	Words about the characters in the story:
Words about the actions in this story:	Words about the story's resolution:
Words that describe the problem:	Other things:

My question about this story:

My prediction about this story:

Introducing the DR-TA and DL-TA Strategies

TARGET
Elementary ✓   Middle School/High School ✓

Asking students to predict what will happen in a story is guaranteed to engage them with the text and sets the scene for teachers to spotlight various literacy fundamentals, including vocabulary, structure, and comprehension. The Predict-O-Gram (see "Introducing the Predict-O-Gram" on page 155) is one strategy that takes advantage of this premise, and DR-TA and DL-TA are two others.

DR-TA, or directed reading-thinking activity, is a teacher-led activity in which students make and then support predictions about a text they are reading. DL-TA, or directed listening-thinking activity, is the same process but involves students listening to the teacher read the text aloud, instead of reading it themselves. DL-TA is a powerful option for the teachers of very beginning readers who are not yet reading on their own, and it can help students learn how to make predictions. Although this strategy can be used with a large group of students, it may be more effective with a smaller group of 6 to 12 students.

To set up the DR-TA or DL-TA, the teacher carefully reviews the text, prepares an introduction that does not give the story away, and selects points at which the students confirm previous predictions and make new ones for the next section.

Students make predictions before and during reading, stopping at the teacher's predetermined points. The teacher's role is to guide students as they make their predictions, asking them to support or contradict their predictions with both information from the text and their own background knowledge. It is important that no one has read the story before or reads ahead. The teacher may direct students to use a piece of paper to cover up the text that comes after the stopping point. After everyone has made their predictions, the class comes together to have a summarizing discussion.

To help teachers organize these activities, literacy coaches can work with them to fill out the DR-TA/DL-TA Planning Sheet. Once teachers are comfortable with the activities, they should complete the sheet themselves. Teachers can also use the sheet to evaluate the lesson.

PART 2

References for further learning

Blachowicz, C., & Ogle, D. (2001). *Reading comprehension: Strategies for independent learners.* New York: Guilford Press.

Stauffer, R. G. (1969). *Directed reading maturity as a cognitive process.* New York: Harper & Row.

GOALS

- To help students feel actively engaged in making meaning of a text.
- To help teachers observe that students are actively monitoring their own comprehension.
- To offer an alternative to teacher-generated or manual-generated questions about a text.

IMPLEMENTATION

1. Identify a learning goal that the teacher wants students to achieve. Discuss whether the teacher will collect the evidence verbally or in writing and how much practice students will have before the evaluation.

2. Based on the learning goal, collaborate to construct an action plan for achieving it. Developing a contract (see "Coaching by Contract" on page 58) to delineate the responsibilities of the teacher and the coach.

3. Collaborate with the teacher to select an appropriate first text to use.

4. Explain the three main procedural steps to the teacher: (1) ask students to make predictions that they can confirm, (2) have students read to confirm or disconfirm their predictions, and (3) lead students in a discussion about their predictions.

5. Help the teacher identify points in the story that most readily lend themselves to prediction. Also identify any challenging points in the text where students could have trouble understanding if they are not monitoring their comprehension. Record these on the DR-TA/DL-TA Planning Sheet and on a handout for students.

6. Based on the selected stopping points, help the teacher construct a brief introduction to the story that will help students get into the text. Document the introduction on the planning sheet.

7. After the activity, meet with the teacher to review the "Challenges" and "Student Response" sections of the sheet to identify areas for improvement and instructional need.

REFLECTION, EVALUATION, AND PLANNING

1. How can you know whether the teacher is ready to conduct the DR-TA/DL-TA discussion without your assistance?

2. How are students responding? Are there trends among students? For example, are their predictions off target more often than not?

3. How is the pace of the student discussions?

4. When necessary, support the teacher in conducting discussions that suggest there are no right answers.

5. How are students listening to each other's predictions? What evidence do you see that they are able to build on each other's statements?

6. Based on teacher response and student outcomes, are there any topics the teacher might want to study with a group of colleagues (see "Planning a Teachers' Study Group" on page 192)?

7. What might be an effective way for the teacher to share student work with colleagues? Could you arrange to have the teacher's classroom available for visitors to observe or could you share student work at grade-level meetings?

DR-TA/DL-TA Planning Sheet

Story Title _____ Date _____

Author _____ DR-TA ☐ DL-TA ☐

Location (anthology, novel, etc.) _____

Introduction:

Stopping Points:

Challenges:

Student Response:

Example DR-TA/DL-TA Planning Sheet

Story Title _Strong John_   Date _11/07_

Author _Joan Chase Bowden_   DR-TA ☐ DL-TA ☒

Location (anthology, novel, etc.) _Classroom library_

Introduction:
- Introduce as a fairy tale—review genre if needed
- Read title to them and ask to look at the pictures
- Prompt for prediction based on title and pictures

Stopping Points:
- End of page 8—Predict what kind of job John might get.
- End of page 14—What do you think John will say to the farmer?
- End of page 25—What kind of job do you think John will get next? Look for notion of previous jobs being on the farm.
- End of page 43—What will John do now? Prompt to use John's previous "solutions" to help them predict.
- End of 49—Predict what the queen will say to John and do for him.
- End of 59—Predict what the queen's "rewards" will be for the three sly people.

Challenges:
- Trouble with word "sly."

Student Response:
- Did well, although many students struggled with identifying the kinds of jobs that take place on a farm.

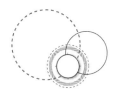

Introducing the Making Words Activity

TARGET

Elementary ✓   Middle School/High School ___

Given the letters M, C, A, E, A, and R, what words can you make? In the Making Words activity, teachers post the letters of a word out of order and ask students to make multiple short words and one longer word that includes all the letters. This helps students think about letters, sounds, words, and spelling patterns in a new way.

Each lesson begins with the teacher posting a large set of letters that make a word into a pocket chart. They then encourage students to think about the letters and sound patterns they know and ask them to make words with two to five letters. For instance, thinking about the silent letter E and chunks such as *–am* and *–ar* could give them *came, am,* and *ram,* along with words such as *are* and *ace.* After having students make 10 to 15 smaller words, teachers challenge them to use all the letters in one large word. In this case, *camera.*

This activity is a fun and powerful way to let students with a wide range of spelling proficiencies engage in the same task. However, it can be a challenge to gather the materials needed, and this is where the literacy coach's assistance can be invaluable. If teachers already have all the resources they need, they'll be more prone to use the activity frequently and more effectively.

There are Web sites, such as www.wordsmith.org/anagram, that provide hundreds of words from which the teacher can select. Search the Internet and compile a list of sites that teachers can use.

For the activity, students need multiple large letters for each word. Teachers need to have a complete set of letters available for each possible word. Some teachers may even choose to make separate letters for each child who struggles with discovering words so that they can work individually. Although letter sets can be used again and again, initial preparation is time-consuming. Literacy coaches can help teachers initially prepare a full alphabet with multiple copies of each letter.

To evaluate how the school is using Making Words, the literacy coach can solicit responses to the Making Words Teacher Survey. Based on the responses, you can decide which topics to present at an inservice workshop (see "Planning a Professional Development Workshop" on page 36) or whether teachers with similar issues should form a study group (see "Planning a Teachers' Study Group" on page 192). The feedback can also help you decide how to allot your time and energy.

References for further learning

Bear, D. R., Invernizzi, M., Templeton, S., & Johnston, F. (2008). *Words their way: Word study for vocabulary and spelling instruction* (3rd ed.). Upper Saddle Creek, NJ: Prentice Hall.

Cunningham, P. M. (2000). *Phonics they use: Words for reading and writing.* New York: Longman.

Cunningham, P. M., & Hall, D. P. (2008). *Making words third grade: 70 hands-on lessons for teaching prefixes, suffixes, and homophones.* Upper Saddle Creek, NJ: Pearson.

Wordsmith.org: www.wordsmith.org/anagram

GOALS

- To provide an alternative method of teaching phonics and high-frequency words.
- To structure whole-group activities that support students with different skill levels.

IMPLEMENTATION

1. In cooperation with the teacher, design a plan that outlines both the teacher's and the coach's roles and the time line. Using a contract (see "Coaching by Contract" on page 58) may be helpful.

2. Use the teacher's knowledge, observations of students, and assessment data to identify one or more student learning goals. For example, students should be able to recognize a particular set of sight words or be able to phonetically spell regular, three-letter words.

3. Determine how to evaluate whether Making Words is meeting the teacher's student learning goals. For example, if the learning goal is increased ability to phonetically spell simple, three-letter words, would a pre- and post-spelling assessment be the best way to evaluate their skills?

4. Select a group of words from a Web site or other resource that contains spelling patterns or will help the teacher achieve the learning goal.

5. Locate funds to purchase a program or use the computer to make the letters and resources needed for each activity.

6. Decide whether the teacher should first complete the activity with small groups to become comfortable it. If so, you may need to help the teacher with the other students until the teacher becomes comfortable with incorporating the whole class in the activities.

REFLECTION, EVALUATION, AND PLANNING

1. Meet with the teacher to look over the supply of source words, letter cards, and so forth. Check to see that they are prepared and organized to make sure the activities go smoothly.
2. How are students moving toward the teacher's learning goal for them? For example, if the goal was to have students improve their knowledge of spelling patterns, is it reflected on the targeted assessment?
3. Which students are not actively engaged when the teacher is working with the whole group? Identify what obstacles stand in their way.
4. What is the time line for ending your support of this activity? Is the teacher getting more comfortable orchestrating the activity and analyzing the results?
5. What is the most effective way to share with the rest of the school? For example, is the teacher comfortable with visitations from other teachers or discussing student work at grade-level meetings?
6. Based on the results of the teacher survey, do you need to establish a Making Words study group (see "Planning a Teachers' Study Group" on page 192)?

Making Words Teacher Survey

To support our primary department's efforts to use Making Words to strengthen spelling and reading, please fill out the form below so that I can know how to support you.

Name _____ Date _____

Grade Level _____ Years of Experience with Making Words _____

	Yes	No	Not Sure
1. I spend between 15–20 minutes each day on a Making Words activity.			
2. The materials I have for Making Words are sufficient.			
3. I can access and print the resources available to me online.			
4. It is currently taking too long to prepare and organize materials for Making Words.			
5. Making Words is benefiting my students' spelling and writing.			
6. I see Making Words has a positive effect on most or many students' abilities to recognize words.			
7. I would like more professional development on aspects of Making Words.			
8. I am struggling to organize and store materials for these activities.			

9. I would appreciate additional support with these aspects of Making Words:

10. Other comments I would like to offer about this word program:

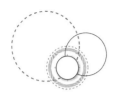

Introducing Interactive Writing

TARGET
Elementary ✓   Middle School/High School ___

A powerful way to combine real-life writing with word study, interactive writing is an instructional activity in which the teacher and students collaborate to write a message.

Interactive writing draws on the interactions of the mentor (teacher) and the apprentice (student) in the language experience approach (see "Using the Language Experience Approach (LEA)" on page 143) and on shared writing. Student's involvement is increased in interactive writing because they share the pen.

After the teacher selects the context for writing—such as a literature response, news, survey, or recipe—the teacher and students orally compose and construct the message together. Next, students write individual words or letters of the message, depending on the grade level and the intent of the lesson.

The teacher carefully selects what students will write, taking into consideration the word's potential instructional value. The spellings of certain words should be beyond students' capacity. For example, if a kindergarten class was writing the message, "We fed bread to the ducks," the teacher might select one student to write the "b" and another student to write the "d" in the word *bread*. Then the teacher writes the "-rea-" because of its irregular spelling pattern. Conventional spelling is always required in interactive writing messages, and correction tape should be available to edit the message as needed.

Once the message is complete, the teacher can read it and post it in the classroom to provide multiple, rich opportunities for rereading. The teacher observes students' writing behaviors during the interactive writing lessons to inform future word study instruction and future interactive writing lessons.

To help the teachers assess the activity and students' learning, literacy coaches can supply the following Interactive Writing Evaluation. Working on interactive writing with a grade-level team who can share their successes and challenges is a particularly beneficial experience for everyone. Study groups are also an excellent setting for bringing teachers together as learners (see "Planning a Teachers' Study Group" on page 192).

References for further learning

McCarrier, A., Fountas, I. C., & Pinnell, G. S. (1999). *Interactive writing: How language and literacy come together, K–2.* Portsmouth, NH: Heinemann.

McGee, L., & Morrow, L. M. (2005). *Teaching literacy in kindergarten: Tools for teaching literacy.* New York: Guilford Press.

GOALS

- To combine real-life writing with word study.
- To draw on the interactions of the teacher and student in the language experience approach and shared writing.
- To increase student involvement in interactive writing.
- To support teachers in planning for future word study activities and interactive writing lessons.

IMPLEMENTATION

1. Engage K–2 teachers in discussions about interactive writing, and invite teachers who have implemented interactive writing to share their experiences.
2. Distribute the Interactive Writing Evaluation and talk about how to use it.
3. Support teachers in writing a plan to implement it in their classrooms. Individual teachers may want customized plans, or teachers may come together and write a plan for their whole grade level.
4. Express your interest in visiting a classroom during an interactive writing lesson.
5. Develop a way to share the work done on interactive writing products. Encourage teachers to each bring one of their interactive writing products to the next grade-level meeting to share how students responded and their rationale for choosing which letters to let students write and which letters to write themselves.
6. Discuss ways to evaluate the effectiveness of the interactive writing products in terms of rereading and types of student involvement.

REFLECTION, EVALUATION, AND PLANNING

1. Identify supplies that teachers need to implement interactive writing. Develop a plan or proposal to apply for funds from the administration.

2. Which books and articles are available in the professional library (see "Building a School's Professional Library" on page 185) to support further inquiry? Topics such as developmental spelling, phonemic awareness, conventions of writing, and concept of words are all well researched and documented, providing articles and even books for a study group to read and discuss.

3. If the teacher is not comfortable sharing this strategy during peer visitations, what other ways can teachers share their work and student outcomes with other staff?

4. Which teachers might welcome a coaching cycle (see "The Coaching Cycle" on page 54) on interactive writing?

Interactive Writing Evaluation

Date _____

Context/Topic _____

Message:

Writing Behaviors Observed

Initial Consonants	Using Print in Environment
Final Consonants	Using Word Wall
Medial Consonants	Letter Formation
Vowels	Directionality
Spacing	Other

Focus for future lessons and word study:

Troubleshooting for Writer's Workshop

TARGET

Elementary ✔   Middle School/High School ✔

Writing workshops are one of the most valuable tools a coach can support, and they can be the center of a language arts program. Workshops provide an organizational framework for instructing student writers and consist of an introductory minilesson followed by a period of extended writing and concluding with writers sharing their work.

The minilesson is based on students' instructional needs, topic choice, idea development, spelling, grammar, and writing genres. Teachers also instruct students on the writing process: prewriting, drafting, revising, editing, and publishing. The process, however, is not set in stone and is often used recursively.

During the writing section of the workshop, students self-select topics for their writing and work on individual pieces over several days or weeks. Extended periods of writing help students build stamina. They keep a record of their writing inspirations in a writer's notebook. At this point, the teacher meets with students individually to talk about their writing, and the students also conduct peer conferences. These conferences give students a format to reflect on their efforts.

The workshop often ends with one of the writers sharing what they have written. This can be a finished piece of writing or a section of a piece. The teacher evaluates students' work based on rubrics that students are familiar with. It's important for teachers to share their grading standards with students so that they can understand how their writing may be judged. The rubrics can also be resources for students to use to improve their writing.

The demands of implementing a writing workshop are greater than traditional language arts lessons that rely on a textbook or teacher's guide. Teachers implementing writing workshops may seek out the support of the literacy coach to help make the writing workshop run more smoothly. This Writing Workshop Self-Assessment can help coaches initiate and moderate discussions about writing workshops.

Reference for further learning

Fletcher, R., & Portalupi, J. (2001). *Writing workshop: The essential guide.* Portsmouth, NH: Heinemann.

GOALS

- To support teachers in identifying their challenges during implementation of writing workshops.
- To collaborate with teachers to fine-tune a writing workshop.

IMPLEMENTATION

1. When teachers solicit support for implementing a writing workshop, ask them to fill out a Writing Workshop Self-Assessment and schedule a conference to discuss the responses.
2. Visit the classroom while the teacher is conducting a writing workshop. Take neutral notes during your visit and share everything you have written with the teacher.
3. Meet with the teacher to develop an action plan that includes learning goals for students. Start with items that can be adjusted quickly and easily, then move to more challenging goals. A coaching contract (see "Coaching by Contract" on page 58) will be useful so that you are clear about goals and the delineation of the coach's and teacher's responsibilities.
4. Make a time line to work on quick wins and longer-term objectives.
5. Schedule a visit to the classroom again to see how the action plan is going. Systematically work through the list and continue to visit the classroom periodically during writing workshops.

REFLECTION, EVALUATION, AND PLANNING

1. Based on the teachers' responses on the Writing Workshop Self-Assessment, on which aspects of the writer's workshop might they need additional professional development?
2. Do teachers need additional materials to successfully implement a workshop?
3. How often are teachers engaging in writer's workshops during the week? How are they scheduling for it within their language arts block?
4. Which teachers might benefit from a coaching cycle (see "The Coaching Cycle" on page 54)? How can you approach them?
5. As the teachers work on their action plans, how can you encourage them to share their work with colleagues? Could you ask a teacher to make a presentation at a grade-level meeting or in a sharing session at a whole-staff meeting?

Writing Workshop Self-Assessment

Identify the degree to which you have established each component of writing workshops.

	Firmly Established	Partially Established	Initiated	Not Initiated Yet
Initial assessment *Initial writing samples have been analyzed to identify the strengths and needs of individual students and the group.*				
Time *Writing workshop is optimally scheduled daily (meets a minimum three times weekly) for 40–60 minutes.*				
Minilessons *Each workshop session includes a minilesson (no more than 10 minutes) based on student needs. Minilessons include a balance of craft, conventions, content, and routine.*				
Choice *Student self-select topics for writing. Student choice is balanced with district requirements.*				
Curriculum *Students are taught to write in a variety of genres for a variety of purposes and audiences.*				
Writing process *Students use the writing process fluidly and recursively.*				
Writing conferences *Each workshop session includes time to conference with individual students about their writing. Notes from conferences are maintained. Peer conferences are established.*				
Sharing *Each workshop includes an opportunity for students to share their writing. There are opportunities for students to share published writing beyond the classroom.*				
Ongoing assessment *Records are maintained on students' daily writing. Writing is assessed using rubrics that are shared with students. Samples of student writing are retained to document growth over time.*				
Management *The workshop follows a predictable routine. Resources are organized and accessible.*				

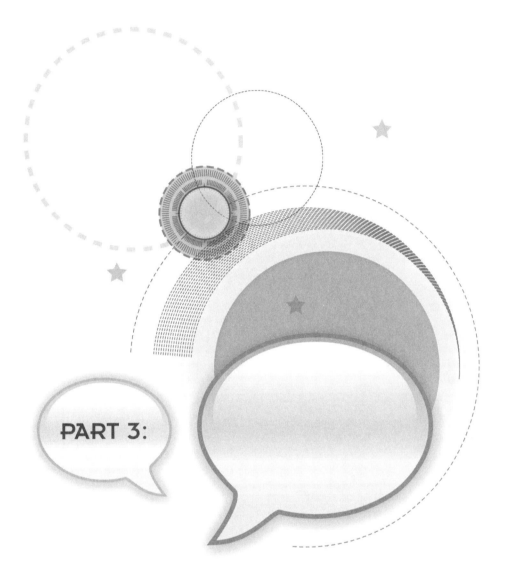

PART 3:

Leadership for a Solid Infrastructure

Communicating with the Principal

TARGET
Elementary ✓   Middle School/High School ✓

A strong principal-coach relationship is critical to the success of literacy coaching, and meeting routinely is one way to forge that relationship. Although each principal-coach team will, over time, forge its own format for meeting, the following Meeting with the Principal chart provides a template for the regularly scheduled meetings between the literacy coach and the principal.

You should establish weekly or biweekly meetings with the principal to discuss the literacy initiatives in the building, the coaching cycles (see "The Coaching Cycle" on page 54) in progress, and what the student learning goals are for those cycles. Other topics could include what study groups (see "Planning a Teachers' Study Group" on page 192) are investigating and how assessment protocols and deadlines are proceeding. Meetings are also a time when the principal and coach look at the building assessments and analyze what they mean in terms of progress and possible professional development. The principal can share central office mandates, budget issues relative to literacy materials, and outcomes from initiatives such as a family reading night (see "Planning a Family Reading Night" on page 221).

The partnership between the principal and the coach is important, but it can also be challenging. For instance, if the principal knows that the coach is working with a teacher who struggles, the principal may be tempted to ask for a report about how that teacher is doing. To protect the relationship with that teacher and the ability to work effectively with all teachers, the coach cannot report on the teacher's status. Instead, many coaches have a set of prepared responses they use to relay the importance of not compromising their teacher relationships.

For example, if asked how Mr. Smith is doing, you might respond: "We're working on guided reading, much like I'm working on it with other teachers. If you'd like to observe how any of these teachers are doing, I can tell you what behaviors to look for. Then you could have a conversation with the teacher after your observation." Another option might be: "Do you want to talk to Mr. Smith about your concerns? Maybe you could set a meeting up." Over time, principals will come to understand the power of a coach's relationships with teachers and are less likely to put you in a position that would jeopardize those relationships.

You need to be as patient in building a relationship with the principal as you are in building relationships with teachers. Over time, the principal will realize that the coach is the principal's advocate with the staff, much as the coach is the staff's advocate with the principal.

GOALS

- To define and build a strong collaborative relationship with the principal.
- To clarify the most effective ways to use a literacy coach.
- To provide a predictable structure for the content of a routine principal-coach meeting.
- To establish the time, place, and length of a routine principal-coach meeting.
- To design a way to document and record topics and decisions discussed at the principal-coach meeting.

IMPLEMENTATION

1. Schedule a meeting with the principal to discuss your partnership. Summer may be a good time to have this meeting, because there may be fewer interruptions and a larger block of time available.
2. Begin the meeting by collecting future agenda items to guide your meetings throughout the school year. These items might include:
   - the principal's hopes for your role
   - the principal's hopes for the school literacy program
   - current literacy initiatives in your building
   - how literacy decisions have been made in your building in the past
   - the role data has played in your building
   - the possibility of establishing a school literacy team
   - the importance of the literacy coach's relationships with teachers in the building
   - describing the types of coaching you can provide

3. Throughout the meeting, take notes and document the important items you discuss. Try using the Meeting with the Principal form; it can serve as the agenda. You can revise it to meet the needs of your meetings.
4. Decide how often you will meet with the principal, aiming for at least one hour per week. Identify who will prepare the agenda, take notes, and make copies for the other.

5. Point out where your weekly schedule will be posted and ask whether the principal wants an individual copy.

REFLECTION, EVALUATION, AND PLANNING

1. What is your current understanding of the principal's vision of your role? Where does it coincide with yours? Are you comfortable addressing any conflicts between your visions of literacy coaching and the principal's?

2. How are your and the principal's roles defined for these meetings? Consider how you will decide what issues will be discussed, who will lead conversations, and how you will approach shared decision making.

3. What issues do you anticipate the principal will want to discuss? Thinking about these issues in advance may be helpful.

4. How have you prioritized issues central to your job as a coach? Be ready to infuse those visions into issues on the agenda.

Meeting with the Principal

Date _____

Long-Range Literacy Goals:
Short-Term Literacy Goals:
Grade-Level/Department Meetings:
Assessment Report:
Current Coaching Cycle:
Study Group/Professional Development Report:
Questions/Comments/Resources Needed:

Next Steps:

Creating a School Literacy Team

TARGET

Elementary ✓   Middle School/High School ✓

Successful schools are places where people work together as a team. To focus on issues of literacy instruction and curriculum, some schools have formed a team consisting of a small, representative group of staff referred to as the *school literacy team* or *building literacy team*. The members of a successful school literacy team can support each other and their colleagues resolve everyday, routine literacy issues, and they can also support each other during major change, such as a new principal.

The principal, teachers who represent each grade level, support staff, and the school's literacy coach often constitute a school literacy team, which meets routinely. While each member plays an important role, the literacy coach is frequently responsible for setting up the team. Early on, your most important job may be to keep reminding everyone that developing an effective school literacy team will not be easy; it will require time and patience, but its rewards will be worth the effort. As time goes by, principals frequently learn to welcome and value the support of the team. At the same time, teachers on the team become proud of their role in supporting their school's literacy development and gain a new level of respect for their principal's role.

Each school's vision for the team may be different. For example, depending on the principal's leadership style, the principal may share leadership and even some of the decision making. But even at schools in which the principal prefers to make most or all decisions, the principal looks to the team for valuable input and advice. Regardless of the form of leadership, the principal, literacy coach, and teachers can come together to assess the school's needs, establish goals and priorities for literacy, and develop a professional development agenda to meet their goals (DeStefano & Hanson, 2007).

In the beginning, teams carefully outline routines, protocols, roles, responsibilities, and a statement of purpose or vision for the school. School literacy team members also serve as liaisons to the rest of the staff, bringing messages and information to grade-level teams, as well as to other school committees, such as parent groups. Over time, the school literacy team begins to tackle important jobs, such as determining whether

ASCD   □ 181

the school has a coherent curriculum across all grades, investigating assessment data to establish needs, and forming study groups (see "Planning a Teachers' Study Group" on page 192) to read about the most current literacy information.

Once you've established a school literacy team, use the following School Literacy Team Survey to assess the team member's attitudes about the effectiveness of the meetings and their work. You can use their responses to plan professional development opportunities and adjust the meeting format.

Reference for further learning

DeStefano, L., & Hanson, M. (2007). *Dimensions of school practice that support and improve student literacy achievement.* Report from the Searle Funds at the Chicago Community Trust.

GOALS

- To demonstrate the important role of a literacy team.
- To establish a literacy vision for the school.
- To develop professional development opportunities that match the school's literacy vision and needs.
- To support the administration by providing multiple voices that represent the staff.
- To create structures to assess and develop plans for cohesive curriculum across grades.
- To build a system for handling change, such as a new principal or new state mandates.

IMPLEMENTATION

1. Meet with the principal to develop a plan for forming a school literacy team based on the considerations listed below.
2. Discuss potential topics for the team to tackle and where leadership might be shared.
3. Consider the size and composition of the team. K–5 buildings may have one member from each grade level, while K–8 buildings may have a single teacher representing multiple grade levels. Will support staff be included?
4. Decide how team members will be chosen. Some schools solicit members, others ask for volunteers. Some use a staff meeting to ask everyone how members could be identified. Those selected for the team should be willing to study, learn, and problem solve in a team setting.
5. Clarify options for meeting times, taking into account contract issues for out-of-school-day meetings and substitute costs. Don't choose the time but do consider options and constraints before letting the team decide.

6. Prepare an agenda for a first meeting that includes the principal's statement about where leadership can be shared, meeting times, and how the team will communicate with staff via note taking and agenda items. Some teams also record a preliminary vision for the team's goals.

7. Survey members after the first or second meeting using the School Literacy Team Survey customized to your needs to document early response and guide future meetings.

REFLECTION, EVALUATION, AND PLANNING

1. How did team members respond to their proposed roles?

2. How did the agenda work? For example, how did time allotments work to cover all topics, review next steps, and construct the next meeting's agenda?

3. How will you handle, collate, and share the surveys with the team so that they can collaborate to work out issues?

4. What trends were suggested by the School Literacy Team Survey? How will you present those trends at the next meeting of the school literacy team?

5. During the meeting, which type of members did most of the talking? How can you make sure that everyone has an equal opportunity to speak? Which similar issues can be handled by the whole team at the next meeting?

6. Which discussions suggested the need to form a learning group around a particular topic?

ASCD ☐ 183

School Literacy Team Survey

Date _____

	Not at All ⟶ Strongly Agree			
	1	2	3	4
1. I felt like my voice was heard today.				
2. I am beginning to understand my role.				
3. The agenda was organized effectively.				

4. What was the best feature of this SLT meeting?

5. What might improve future SLT meetings?

6. Other comments I wish to offer:

Building a School's Professional Library

TARGET

Elementary ✔   Middle School/High School ✔

The heart of professional development in a school is a professional library. It is the literacy coach's first stop when planning professional development sessions, and it is where teachers turn when they have a question or are in search of new strategies or ideas. When teachers want to view footage of instruction or forms of professional development, such as literature discussion groups in action, guided-reading lessons, or team meetings, literacy coaches can also hold grade-level meetings in the professional library.

Good professional libraries are well organized, easy to use, accessible, inviting, and well stocked. Whether you are starting off with a small collection of books on a back shelf in the school library or several bookcases filled with the most current books in the coach's resource room, the Professional Library Inventory Checklist can help you think about how to make your school's professional library the go-to place when staff have questions.

Frequently, literacy coaches have limited funds, and you'll most likely need to be resourceful when stocking the professional library. Ideally, the school's budget will have a permanent line devoted to the professional library. If the library is new, you may need to create a long-term plan for developing it. A viable option may be a five-year plan with larger initial expenditures to set up the library and smaller amounts to maintain it. A deep and careful analysis of what already exists and a five-year plan for enriching the library can be the basis for a detailed discussion with the school principal during budget time.

GOALS

- To critically analyze the existing professional library.
- To make a systematic plan for enhancement and improvements.
- To build a viable professional library to support the coach's, administrators', and teachers' professional learning.

IMPLEMENTATION

1. Get at least one professional book in each of the primary, intermediate, and upper levels or for each curriculum department. Make a plan for acquiring additional books.
2. Devote several days after school to labeling and organizing the professional library.
3. Survey teachers (classroom and special teachers), librarians, and administrators for professional topics of interest.
4. Fill out the Professional Library Inventory Checklist.
5. Highlight the areas marked "No," and prioritize the needs of the library.
6. Immediately begin work on the quick wins. Review recent issues of the professional articles, and make copies of articles related to current issues in your school. Put the articles in laminated, colored folders and place a list of the copied articles in teachers' mailboxes. Make multiple copies of articles on issues of interest to specific grade levels, and bring the copies to the next grade-level meeting.
7. Create a plan—spanning multiple years if necessary—to acquire the resources the library lacks. Systematically work through the list.
8. Meet with the principal to plan a budget for obtaining big-ticket items, such as a computer, DVD player, or monitor.
9. Host an open house when the work is completed and solicit feedback from the staff to assess the value of the resources and create a wish list of additional topics or titles.

REFLECTION, EVALUATION, AND PLANNING

1. How can you generate and maintain interest in the professional library?
2. How much money should be devoted annually to the professional library?
3. What do you need to do to keep the library functional, useful, up-to-date, and organized within the confines of your schedule?
4. How can you arrange your schedule to provide a period a month for library maintenance? Who else might help with the clerical side of the professional library?
5. How can you stay abreast of new books and videos? Can you form a network with other coaches to share the responsibility of staying abreast of new professional books?
6. Are there videos available for the most circulated books?

Professional Library Inventory Checklist

Date _____

	Yes	No
1. Are there at least five books focused on instruction for each grade-level group?		
2. Are there professional journals for each core instructional area?		
3. Are there at least three instructional videotapes for each grade-level group?		
4. Do current books represent all areas of reading and language arts—including writing, read-alouds, guided reading, reading workshops, word study, children's and young adults' literature, content-area reading, comprehension, management, fluency, early literacy, spelling, and assessment?		
5. Do you have multiple copies of books for book clubs or study groups?		
6. Do you feature uses of children's and young adults' literature for instructional purposes (e.g., mentor text for writing or books for modeling comprehension processes)?		
7. Have you weeded out books on outdated practices?		
8. Do you have books about struggling learners for all grade-level groups?		
9. Do you have books on working with English language learners?		
10. Do you have a manageable checkout system?		
11. Do you highlight journal articles that address relevant school issues?		
12. Is your library's organization clear and supportive to users?		
13. Is there comfortable seating for teachers to sit and browse?		
14. Is there a computer in your professional library with useful sites saved as favorites?		
15. Is there a system in place for teachers to request additional titles?		
16. Do you do book talks at faculty and grade-level meetings to introduce new books systematically added to the professional library?		
17. Do you have display areas featuring authors, teacher recommendations, reviews, and so forth?		
18. Do you have nonprofessional books, such as novels and informational books, to encourage teachers to read?		
19. Is there room to expand your library?		
20. Are you systematically adding new titles to your collection?		

Organizing Grade-Level and Department Meetings

TARGET
Elementary ✓   Middle School/High School ✓

Many schools set aside time for grade-level, team, or department meetings, usually arranging for teachers to be relieved of their duties to attend. Many literacy coaches are charged with the task of organizing, convening, and moderating these meetings.

Ripe with potential, these meetings are the perfect forum for teachers working with students at the same grade level or in the same subject area to plan, coordinate, work, study, and learn together. Often, within the group teachers have a variety of talents and strengths and can serve as resources to each other. In short, grade-level or department meetings are an opportunity for teachers working toward the same standards and goals to develop strategies for improving the quality of instruction for their students. Literacy coaches can also capitalize on these meetings to provide grade-level or subject-specific professional development.

Sometimes schools schedule specials or hire substitute teachers to accommodate grade-level, team, or department meetings. However, if time cannot be allocated during the regular school day, these meetings might take place before or after school.

To prevent these meetings from being dominated by housekeeping issues, such as planning field trips, literacy coaches play an important role in keeping teachers focused on student learning and the instruction needed for that learning. Maintaining an agenda can help keep meetings on track, and past agendas and meeting minutes can become a resource for future planning. The following Meeting Minutes template provides a standardized format and starting point for this record keeping.

At periodic times in the year, especially with a newly formed team, teachers can benefit from reflecting on the effectiveness and efficiency of their team meetings. Literacy coaches can prompt discussion by asking questions such as, How can we ensure that student learning goals are at the center of our meetings? and How can we handle some of the housekeeping items differently so that we can spend more time talking about students and instruction?

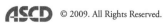

Sometimes, the literacy coach will eventually delegate the job of running the meeting to a teacher in the department or grade level. However, you should continue to attend the meetings and be an ongoing resource for the group.

GOALS

- To plan and organize grade-level, team, or department meetings that focus on student learning and instruction.
- To document actions and decisions made at grade-level, team, or department meetings.
- To help ensure that grade-level, team, or department meetings are an efficient use of time and progress over time.

IMPLEMENTATION

1. Schedule the meeting at the appointed time and notify teachers.
2. Survey teachers (or consult previous team agenda goals) to determine items for the agenda, and prepare an agenda prior the meeting.
3. Make copies of the agenda and distribute them to meeting participants two to three days prior to the meeting. Also retain copies of the agenda to distribute at the meeting as needed.
4. At the meeting, record the names of the meeting participants and those who are absent.
5. Keep a record or the minutes of the meeting, actions to be taken, and goals for the next meeting.
6. Retain a copy of the completed meeting form in a binder stored in an area accessible to administrators and teachers. (Some principals require notes and agendas to be sent to them after the meetings.)

REFLECTION, EVALUATION, AND PLANNING

1. How do you determine whether the form was helpful to keep the meeting focused and participants on task? Attending grade-level meetings may not provide enough information, so consider directly asking teachers about the agenda form.
2. Do you need to revise the minute form to fit grade-level needs?
3. How would you describe individual participation? If there are team members who do not participate, how can you encourage involvement? Consider discussing meeting protocols and individual participation at a whole-staff meeting.

 189

4. How would you describe the respect accorded to each member? Some teams may need support on how to reach consensus.

5. Was student learning a focus of a substantial portion of the meeting? If not, how can you guide the discussion toward student learning goals?

6. How does the agenda work relative to the amount of time available? Time notations and outcomes listed on the agenda can help keep the meetings moving.

7. What kind of grade-level or department-level meeting topics surfaced that need additional support or professional development? Can time be allowed at the team meeting to read a small section of an article or watch a video related to that topic? Or can you introduce study groups (see "Planning a Teachers' Study Group" on page 192) and schedule them for another time? Will the principal purchase study materials?

Meeting Minutes

_____

School

☐ Grade-Level Meeting ☐ Department Meeting

Grade Level or Department _____ Date _____

Chairperson _____ Minutes Submitted By _____

Those in Attendance _____   _____

                                           _____   _____

                                           _____   _____

                                           _____   _____

Absent Members _____

                                      _____

Instructional focus (writing, vocabulary, reading in the content areas, guided reading, etc.):

Goals for this meeting:

Student learning goal(s) discussed:

Minutes:

Topic(s) for next agenda:

Source: Adapted with permission from the work of Kay Connley, literacy coach at Murphy School, Chicago, Ill.

PART 3

Planning a Teachers' Study Group

TARGET

Elementary ✔   Middle School/High School ✔

Traditional thinking was that literacy coaches could simply tell teachers what they should know, and teachers would acquire that new information. Although there is preliminary information that coaches can tell teachers, the deep learning takes place when teachers act on that preliminary information and recognize aspects of the topic particularly relevant to them.

One way the literacy coach can enable that kind of teacher learning is to invite interested teachers to join a study group about a topic. Study groups usually consist of some reading, some discussion, an occasional video, and frequent sharing of student work. How often study groups meet can differ depending on the topic and group members, but to be effective, each meeting should follow an established routine.

Topics for study groups can surface during any teacher interactions with literacy coaches, such as a question at a grade-level meeting or follow-up to a coaching cycle. Frequently, coaches plant the seeds for a study group during a whole-school presentation about a particular topic that appeared frequently on teacher surveys, an area of need identified by school assessment data, or a district mandate for new forms of instruction or curriculum (see "Planning a Professional Development Workshop" on page 36).

After the literacy coach has identified a topic that interests multiple teachers, the coach brings together specific groups of teachers to meet on a regular basis for a limited amount of time. During these meetings, the coach should assume the role of a learner within the group, instead of acting as an expert. Over time, this builds the kind of trust that exists between people learning together.

References for further learning

Allen, J., Szymusiak, K., & Sibberson, F. (2006). *Becoming a literacy leader: Supporting learning and change.* Portland, ME: Stenhouse.

Sweeney, D. (2003). *Learning along the way: Professional development by and for teachers.* Portland, ME: Stenhouse.

GOALS

- To allow teachers to have more control of learning topics that interest them.
- To structure study groups in ways that provide a predictable, safe, nonevaluative, rich climate for learning.
- To bring teachers together in learning groups that create bonds between staff.
- To create a new role for the literacy coach as a colearner with teachers and other staff.

IMPLEMENTATION

1. Confer and plan with the principal to understand guidelines for inviting teachers to join study groups. You should clarify contract issues about whether stipends must be involved; what is considered voluntary; and a reasonable budget for professional materials, such as books and DVDs, to be used at the meetings.
2. If you have a school literacy team (see "Creating a School Literacy Team" on page 181) in place, present the topic of study groups for its input and guidance.
3. Construct an announcement that includes

   - Topics available for study (begin with only one or two groups). Include an explanation of how the topic was chosen, such as by survey or data analysis.
   - Dates, times, and location of the meetings.
   - An explanation of the format for studying together: reading at the meeting itself, discussion, sharing ideas, plans for what they might put into practice, and sharing student work.

4. Select, plan, and purchase a variety of resources that group participants can read, watch, and share at each meeting. These could be short segments of videos or short book chapters. Also purchase treats and drinks, especially for after-school study groups.
5. If study groups do not attract volunteers, approach teachers with whom you already have relationships and ask them to start the ball rolling as a favor.
6. To guide your planning for each study group, complete the Planning a Study Group tool.

REFLECTION, EVALUATION, AND PLANNING

1. How did the first study group participants respond to this type of learning experience?
2. Can you prompt the more quiet participants to add to the discussion? If not, can you ask questions such as, What are your thoughts on this?, to prompt them to participate? Some members will take longer than others to participate actively and should be respected.
3. What did you learn from the first study group that will help you to plan for subsequent study groups?
4. Do you need to revise your agenda—for example, add more time for discussion or time for teachers to read or reread on-site—to be successful?

ASCD 193

Planning a Study Group

Topic _____

Number of Meetings _____ Dates _____

Meeting Times _____ Location _____

Resources:

Meeting Structure for This Topic

Time Allotted	Activity

Notes:

Planning a Study Group Example

Topic *Revision in writing*

Number of Meetings _____4_____ Dates *1/11, 1/25, 2/8, 2/22*

Meeting Times *2:45–4:00* Location *Room 319*

Resources 1. DVD: *The Craft of Grammar: Integrated Instruction in Writer's Workshop*—Jeff Anderson
(Three 5-minute segments that target revision)

2. BOOK: *The Revision Toolbox: Teaching Techniques That Work*—Georgia Heard (Chapter 6)

3. JOURNAL ARTICLE: "I'll Do It My Way: Three Writers and Their Revision Practices"—Stephanie Dix (RT)

Meeting Structure for This Topic

Time Allotted	Activity
15 minutes	reflection/sharing (student samples)
15 minutes	reading article or chapter
10 minutes	discussing article or chapter
10 minutes	watching DVD
10 minutes	discussing response to DVD
15 minutes	action plans for implementation

Notes:

- Five teachers. First two sessions—a challenge: Two people dominated. Asked quieter ones, What do you think? Helped with one.

- Next time, try graphic organizer to write thoughts during reading and DVD.

- Quiet one brought great student samples and asked for coaching cycle on revision.

- Two teachers came unprepared. I stressed that they are still welcome and we read on-site, too. One started to come prepared.

- Four of them want to do another study group.

- Materials worked well. They really liked DVD segments. Next time, try watching segments twice because so much to see on tape.

- Have to stay silent and let them talk more.

- Wonder if I could do this in an hour . . . ?

Forming a Teacher Book Club

TARGET

Elementary ✔   Middle School/High School ✔

When teachers meet to discuss a book, they build camaraderie and a sense of community. The literacy coach is in an excellent position to organize professional or nonprofessional book clubs for teachers.

A teacher book club can take various forms and have a number of purposes. Of course, the teachers can discuss a professional book to help them meet the instructional needs of their students, but they can also take away important lessons from other types of reading. For example, Ellin Oliver Keene and Susan Zimmerman (2007) led teachers in book discussions of novels, short stories, and poetry to help them better understand reading comprehension.

If teachers read and discuss a young adult or children's book, such as *Harry Potter and the Sorcerer's Stone,* by J. K. Rowling, they can gain insight into its appeal to their students. Reading a challenging novel can help teachers build empathy for struggling readers and examine their own reading processes. If possible, seek a funding source for the book club's first book; teachers should be willing to buy their own books once the practice catches on.

When organizing a book club, try to offer meetings at different times to help accommodate the staff's schedules. Some literacy coaches have found that a grade-level meeting (see "Organizing Grade-Level and Department Meetings" on page 188) is a perfect venue for methodically reading through a professional book. You may also consider holding the meeting before or after the school day. To give the meeting a more social atmosphere, you can bring snacks or ask for volunteers to supply them. A before-school book club can include coffee and bagels. If you choose to have an after-school book club, you might consider meeting somewhere outside the school. Some teachers find it easier to concentrate on the discussion when they are not in such close proximity to their classrooms.

If the teachers are having trouble finding time to finish longer books, a good choice may be a picture book with universal appeal or one with instructional implications, such as *The Dot,* by Peter H. Reynolds. For clubs that read novels, you may want to select a quicker, light read for the first meeting. Some coaches even build in time at the book club meeting for teachers to read.

Even if teachers occasionally come to the book club meetings without reading the book, be welcoming and accepting of their efforts to attend. Hopefully, they'll be prepared for the next session and come to appreciate learning from a professional book or just enjoying a novel—in the company of their colleagues and literacy coach. The following Book Club Plan tool can help you keep track of the selections and attendees and evaluate the discussion to modify future meetings as needed.

Reference for further learning

Keene, E. O., & Zimmerman, S. (2007). *A mosaic of thought: The power of comprehension strategy instruction* (2nd ed.). Portsmouth, NH: Heinemann.

GOALS

- To plan and organize a teacher book club.
- To promote lifelong literacy and reflection on one's own reading process.
- To build community and trust among teachers.
- To model engaged reading among teachers.

IMPLEMENTATION

1. Select an appropriate book to meet the goal of the group.
2. Announce the book club by posting flyers, distributing flyers to teachers' mailboxes, and making announcements at staff and grade-level meetings.
3. Form a group of four to eight teachers. Groups of more than eight may limit opportunities to talk, so you may need more than one group.
4. At the first meeting, decide together how you will pace the reading of the book and ask for volunteers to facilitate chapter discussions and bring snacks.
5. Record the information you discussed on the Book Club Plan, and distribute the sheet to the group at the next meeting.
6. Put reminders in teachers' mailboxes the day before the book club meetings.
7. At the final meeting, ask teachers to fill out an evaluation of the book club. You can use their feedback to inform future sessions.

REFLECTION, EVALUATION, AND PLANNING

1. Are all book club members actively participating? If not, what can you do to offer more opportunities for the quiet participants?

2. Would this group benefit from a more structured format?

3. If you are using a professional book, do teachers see this as collaborative or as instruction from you? Can you modify the format of the meetings to make them more collaborative?

4. How can the book club provide teachers with opportunities to reflect on what they learn about themselves as readers to support their students?

5. If teachers came unprepared, what can you do to support them? Should you build in time for reading during the book club meeting? Should you require teachers to read a shorter selection for the next meeting?

6. How can you find funding to purchase the materials?

7. What kind of book club experiences should you offer in the future?

8. What did teacher evaluations reveal about the effectiveness of the book club? What revisions are you going to make to improve the next book club?

Book Club Plan

Participants:

1. _____ 5. _____

2. _____ 6. _____

3. _____ 7. _____

4. _____ 8. _____

Title _____

Author _____

Type of Book _____

Facilitator _____ Snack Provider _____

Date _____ Pages Read _____

Notes:

Facilitator _____ Snack Provider _____

Date _____ Pages Read _____

Notes:

Facilitator _____ Snack Provider _____

Date _____ Pages Read _____

Notes:

PART 3

Analyzing Primary Classroom Resources

TARGET

Elementary ✓   Middle School/High School __

Teachers cannot be expected to implement a program if they do not have the critical materials and resources. Similarly, newer teachers shouldn't be expected to implement the same level of instruction if they have significantly fewer materials than more experienced colleagues at their grade level. This disparity is especially evident at the primary level, at which time students read more, shorter books and when students need more writing implements because they are not as facile as older students. For this reason, literacy coaches should consider surveying the school's resources and materials at the primary level.

You can begin by studying the school's literacy program and collaborating with teachers at each grade level to ascertain the supplies they need to move their students forward to conventional reading and writing. Then you can create an inventory of the resources teachers have. The following Students' Reading and Writing Materials Inventory and Teachers' Instructional Supports Inventory tools can help you keep track of classroom resources. Although it may take weeks—or in some cases, months—to gather all the information initially, you can maintain the inventory efficiently.

Before beginning this survey, the literacy coach needs to collaborate with the principal to garner support and come to a shared understanding of budgetary allowances. Once the survey is complete, the coach meets with the principal again. At this point, you can share a prioritized summary of what is needed; how many of the items are one-time purchases; and what is an ongoing, consumable resource. If possible, provide some ballpark figures, although a clerk may be better suited to that task. The principal may then be able to give some sense of how long it will take to bring the primary grades up to speed.

Creating the inventory and procuring the needed materials are important, but the survey process also has other benefits. The coach's work on behalf of the teachers builds positive relationships because you are clearly advocating on their behalf. By working with the principal, you both better understand each other's needs. Finally, the process gives the coach a window into the primary teachers' understandings of the importance of these resources and how they are used, which may reveal professional development needs.

GOALS

- To discover the availability of materials necessary for primary teachers to implement the school's literacy program at those grade levels.
- To develop a systematic and equitable approach to acquiring instructional resources for literacy.
- To develop a plan of advocating for permanent budget allowances for resources critical to implementing the literacy program at the primary level.

IMPLEMENTATION

1. Meet with the principal to confirm the importance of resources for an effective primary literacy program and gain support to conduct your survey. Collaborate to decide the best approach to collecting this information. It could be helpful to schedule this meeting for summer or before a budget deadline.
2. In grade-level teams, determine which materials are critical for implementing your literacy program. If they are not listed on the sheet, revise it to include them.
3. Schedule appointments across two to four weeks to meet with teachers to fill out the form. You may need to meet during specials or before or after school.
4. Record the information on the chart, distinguishing nonconsumables from consumables.
5. As you complete each grade level, schedule a grade-level meeting to analyze the needs and prioritize the list in case the budget necessitates multiple years to bring classrooms up-to-date.
6. After completing all K–2 classrooms, meet with the principal again to discuss your findings. Attaching dollar amounts to your list before this meeting may facilitate the discussion.
7. With the principal's support, make a budget and a schedule for systematically acquiring new resources and replacing consumable resources on a yearly basis or as needed.
8. As resources are acquired, record them on the chart with the date.

REFLECTION, EVALUATION, AND PLANNING

1. Reflecting on the process, was there anything that you would have changed? Why and how?
2. Were needs localized at a specific grade level or with individual teachers? How can you further support the needs?
3. Do you need additional funding, beyond the building's capacity, to accommodate the important resources needed? How can you secure this funding?
4. How did this analysis inform future professional development sessions?

K–2 Students' Reading and Writing Materials Inventory

Key: 0 = Not applicable
1 = Little or no resources
2 = Emerging capacity
3 = Acceptable resources

Grade	Teacher	Guided-Reading Little Books	Take-Home Library	Independent Reading Library	Big Book Library

Grade	Teacher	Poetry Library	Listening Centers	Reading for Meaning	Student Journals	Dry-Erase Boards, Markers, Erasers

K–2 Teachers' Instructional Supports Inventory

Key: 0 = Not applicable
     1 = Little or no resources
     2 = Emerging capacity
     3 = Acceptable resources

Grade	Teacher	Easel	Chart Tablet (10)	Chart Paper	Pocket Chart Holder	Pocket Charts	Sentence Strips	Magnetic Boards

Grade	Teacher	Magnetic Letters	Wikki Stix	Sticky Notes	Framing Cards	Pointers	Transparencies	Storage Materials

PART 3

Analyzing Classroom Libraries

TARGET

Elementary ✓   Middle School/High School ___

At the core of literacy instruction is a rich classroom library. Although many teachers know this statement to be true, district and school budgets do not always acknowledge the value of a classroom library. It's important for literacy coaches to advocate for classroom libraries, and informal surveys of classroom libraries can kick off that effort.

Literacy coaches can visit classrooms and note the books the libraries contain, their appropriateness for the grade level, how they are stored in the room, and how they are arranged in terms of genre and level of challenge. You can also note whether there are enticing displays to prompt children to read. The classroom library should be an exciting place from which students can choose a book. Perhaps the most challenging and complex aspect of a classroom library is how the teacher uses the library to both stimulate reading and connect to instruction and literacy curriculum.

With the Classroom Library Inventory Checklist, the literacy coach can work with teachers to answer a set of questions about the quality, quantity, and structure of the teacher's classroom library. Based on the results of the checklist, you can create easy, short-term action plans, such as displaying books differently so that they attract more attention, and more challenging long-term action plans, such as working to increase knowledge about the importance classroom libraries both with the teacher and those who hold the purse strings in a district.

Although classroom libraries can be expanded by accepting free books offered to students from commercial publishers, these books may not be the ones that the classroom library desperately needs. The content of classroom libraries should closely align with the school's literacy curriculum and content areas.

Teachers will most likely be grateful for your help making their classroom libraries exciting places for students, and the interaction will nurture a strong relationship between the literacy coach and the teacher.

GOALS

- To provide a framework for the teacher and coach to examine classroom libraries.
- To develop a plan for increasing the quantity of books in classroom libraries.
- To develop classroom libraries that support quality literacy instruction.
- To provide classroom libraries that encourage, support, and inspire students to read for both pleasure and information.

IMPLEMENTATION

1. Meet with the principal to discuss the need to examine the quantity and quality of classroom libraries in your building.
2. Ask teachers if you can visit their rooms to look at their classroom libraries. Note the quantities, how they are arranged and presented, whether there are adjacent areas for student reading, and so forth.
3. Revise the Classroom Library Inventory Checklist to make sure it matches the needs at your school.
4. Find one teacher or pair who will collaborate with you to examine their library, and use the Classroom Library Inventory Checklist to identify that library's strengths and needs.
5. Collaborate with the teacher to make immediate, low-cost and no-cost changes, such as modifying organization, weeding out books, creating displays, or changing the library's location.
6. Develop a plan for acquiring new books. It may have to cover multiple years. Consider arranging for teacher loans from the public library until the teacher's own collection is complete. Be aware that there can be risks, such as lost books and confusion about which books are the library's, to adding public library books to the classroom collection.
7. Support the teacher in developing an instructional plan to teach and help students learn how to use the library most effectively.
8. Spotlight the library as it begins to change with before and after pictures.
9. Give surveys to students before and after the changes to document their responses.
10. Consider preparing a narrative, with pictures and student surveys, describing the change in the room. Use the report to lobby school and district administrators to consider a permanent budget line for classroom libraries.
11. Invite other teachers to visit the newly revitalized classroom libraries.
12. Evaluate teachers' participation in school book clubs, such as Scholastic and Trumpet. Create handouts to inform teachers about the options for such clubs.

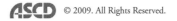

13. Investigate the possibility of a book fair that would use some of the profits to support classroom libraries.

14. Approach the school-parent organization about funding for classroom libraries. You can use the narrative report that you developed for administrators.

REFLECTION, EVALUATION, AND PLANNING

1. How can you share the work on libraries with other teachers? Can they show before and after pictures at a staff meeting or make a presentation at a local conference?

2. Based on your insights from the collaboration with the first teacher, can you revise the checklist or process for the future?

3. How could the first teacher inspire other teachers to form a study group (see "Planning a Teachers' Study Group" on page 192) focusing on classroom libraries?

Classroom Library Inventory Checklist

	Yes	No
1. Are there at least 10 books per child in your classroom library?		
2. Does the readability of your library span two years above to two years below grade level?		
3. Have you taught your students how to select "just right" books?		
4. Does your classroom library include a variety of fiction genres?		
5. Do informational books make up at least one-third of your collection?		
6. Does your library contain at least 5 to 10 poetry books?		
7. Does your library contain at least 5 books of at least three popular series appropriate for your grade level?		
8. Are some of your books displayed with covers facing outward?		
9. Does your library include display areas featuring authors, student recommendations, and so forth?		
10. Is the library's organization clear, explicit, and manageable for students?		
11. Do you have a manageable checkout system?		
12. Is your library located in an area of the classroom that is accessible, yet conducive to reading?		
13. Is there comfortable seating in the library area?		
14. Is there room to expand the library?		
15. Are you using sturdy, secure shelving?		
16. Are you systematically adding new titles to your collection?		
17. Do you give book talks for each new book added to the library?		
18. Do you periodically weed out books from your collection?		
19. Do you include time for independent reading in your day?		
20. Do you use your classroom library to support instruction across the curriculum?		

First three action priorities for your library:

1. _____

2. _____

3. _____

PART 3

Organizing a Literacy Closet

TARGET

Elementary ✔   Middle School/High School ✔

Why should I put all of my student books in a centralized school literacy closet? This is a common—and fair—question teachers ask when literacy coaches first suggest creating a literacy closet. A literacy closet is a room in which all leveled student books and magazines are stored, and all teachers have access to all books. Teachers can check them out as needed and return them when finished.

Experienced literacy coach Debbie Blanco, whose building has had a literacy closet for more than 10 years, believes it serves two important functions:

- The money spent on books goes farther. Instead of only serving one grade level or one group of students, the books can be used in multiple classrooms and by multiple grade levels.
- It prompts everyone to develop a common language for leveling books and describing the reading level of the students who read them.

To start a literacy closet, the staff must agree to differentiate instruction by reading levels. Literacy closets are designed to serve teachers who have broken their students into small groups of students reading at different levels. Teachers then attempt to provide books that closely match the reading level of the students in a group. If everyone in a class is reading from the same book, there is little reason for a literacy closet.

Another prerequisite for a literacy closet is solid support from the administration. If the principal does not support the idea, it is unlikely there will be a budget to add books or that you will have the room and supplies needed to manage the closet. Literacy coaches may also need some clerical help to manage the closet. You may consider requesting the help of a paraprofessional aide for one hour each day to keep the books in the closet organized, shelved, and labeled.

The success of a literacy closet depends on the involvement of teachers. Before you start the closet, consider forming a small literacy closet advisory board with representatives from different grade levels. This group will provide critical input for how the literacy closet is functioning and become the public relations arm that introduces the concept and organization to the rest of the staff.

The following Literacy Closet Checklist can guide you in creating this valuable resource.

References for further learning

Fountas, I. C., & Pinnell, G. S. (2005). *The Fountas & Pinnell leveled book list, K–8* (2006–2008 ed.). Portsmouth, NH: Heinemann.

Pinnell, G. S., & Fountas, I. C. (1996). *Guided reading: Good first teaching for all children.* Portsmouth, NH: Heinemann.

GOALS

- To establish a room where all teachers have access to all leveled books.
- To balance supplies of fiction and nonfiction leveled books and student magazines.
- To identify an efficient and workable organization and checkout system.

IMPLEMENTATION

1. Meet with the principal to discuss the possibility of developing a literacy closet. During the meeting, request one hour of clerical support per day so that you can remain free to work with teachers before, during, and after school.
2. Develop a multiple-year funding plan for adding books and magazines to the closet, with an emphasis on balancing inequities between fiction and content-area leveled texts and between primary- and upper-grade books.
3. Present the concept of a literacy closet to the staff and ask for volunteers to form a literacy closet advisory board. If you have a school literacy team (see "Creating a School Literacy Team" on page 181), it can fill this role.
4. Arrange to visit established literacy closets in other districts or buildings, accompanied by members of the advisory board.
5. Work with the advisory board and administration to choose a leveling system to follow in classrooms and in the literacy closet. Many schools use the Fountas and Pinnell system because you can purchase books that already have a designated reading level.
6. Develop a gradual, multiple-year plan for opening the literacy closet. Consider asking certain teachers to be the first literacy closet contributors by sending their own leveled books to be housed in the literacy closet. Also survey teachers to find out who will be the first literacy closet users, those checking out books to use in their rooms.

7. Develop a system for checking out and returning books. Look into the experiences of buildings and coaches with existing, well-functioning literacy closets.

8. Arrange for an open house when the closet is ready, and invite all teachers to see where it is and how it works.

9. After the literacy closet has been open for a month, distribute a survey to teachers asking for feedback on the new resource.

10. At the end of the year, ask teachers to fill out a survey about the quantity and quality of resources as well as the organization and checkout system. Make changes based on their feedback.

REFLECTION, EVALUATION, AND PLANNING

1. Is it possible that the literacy closet takes valuable time away from your work with teachers? If so, who can you ask for assistance once the closet is open and functioning?

2. How is the checkout system working? Can you streamline the process to make the library more successful? What rules are in place for how long books can be kept?

3. What trends surfaced on your end-of-year survey? Did teachers identify level shortages or suggest improvement to the organization or checkout system?

4. How is your advisory board functioning? How often should it meet?

5. Does the way teachers use the closet suggest the need for targeted professional development? Should you arrange for discussions about particular groups of students? For example, are teachers checking out fewer books for struggling readers, thereby giving them less volume of reading than more proficient readers?

Literacy Closet Checklist

	Done	Notes/Follow-Up Needed
1. Meet with principal to discuss: • rationale and goals of literacy closet • routine yearly funding • clerical support to keep coach free for teachers • location		
2. Make an informational presentation to staff about the literacy closet.		
3. Solicit volunteers for literacy closet advisory board.		
4. Visit established literacy closets with members of advisory board.		
5. Identify the most efficient leveling system to use in the closet.		
6. Work with advisory board to develop an organization plan, including book storage, identification, and a checkout system.		
7. Survey teachers to determine underrepresented levels.		
8. Order materials needed for closet, such as storage bins.		
9. Set up closet for books.		
10. Collect books to be stored in closet.		
11. Train paraprofessional to reshelve books.		
12. Invite teachers to an open house to showcase literacy closet.		
13. Establish monthly meetings of advisory board.		
14. Distribute survey for preliminary feedback after the closet is open one month.		
15. Distribute end-of-year survey.		
16. Meet with advisory board to plan for next year.		

Notes:

PART 3

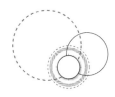

Sponsoring School Visitations

TARGET
Elementary ✓   Middle School/High School ✓

One successful and popular way for literacy coaches to provide professional development is to arrange for the teachers to visit classrooms at other schools. Teachers who agree to be visited are sometimes referred to as *laboratory teachers,* because they and their literacy coaches are currently working on one or more literacy practices and are willing to share their efforts. Literacy coaches report that teachers are more willing to visit and be visited by teachers from other schools than those from their own school.

To make the visitation productive, both schools should have some common goals and teachers should visit classrooms working on issues similar to theirs. For instance, a common reason for primary teachers to visit each other is because both schools are working on guided reading. For middle and high schools, teachers may be working on content-area reading and writing.

Literacy coaches should also consider whether the context of the visiting and host classrooms is similar. For instance, coaches report that a visiting teacher with a class size of 29 students who observes a teacher with only 19 students has difficulty distinguishing between what is made possible as a result of the teacher's literacy work and what is made possible by a smaller class size. Other demographics, such as the percentage of English language learners and number of students with free- and reduced-price lunch, can also be important.

However, the challenge with cross-school visitations is that they bring together teachers who do not know each other and who are not familiar with the context of each other's classrooms. A school brochure is one way to introduce your school to visitors or the laboratory teachers. It describes the context into which the initiative or classroom strategy fits, and it can range from a simple, one-page description to a pamphlet complete with color photos. The literacy coach can collaborate with the school literacy team (see "Creating a School Literacy Team" on page 181) or a group of representatives from each grade level to identify school highlights that would be important for visitors.

Having teachers exchange letters of introduction is another way for them to familiarize themselves with the host or visiting teachers and their classrooms. The introductory letter is intended to present some of teacher's background as well as classroom characteristics, such as demographics and size. This allows the visiting and host teachers to understand what they might and might not have in common.

Literacy coaches can facilitate the letter exchange by providing teachers with the following Visitation Introduction Form and ensuring that the completed forms are sent to the partner school. When it comes time for the visitation, you can help teachers keep track of their observations with the Visiting Teacher Observation Form (see "Using a Visitation Observation Form" on page 217).

GOALS

- To provide visiting teachers with a written introduction to the teachers and coaches who are participating in cross-school visitations.
- To increase the comfort level of teachers who have not worked together in the past but who plan to visit each other's classrooms.
- To help the literacy coaches moderate the discussions before and after classroom observations.
- To provide context and background to make classroom observation as productive as possible.

IMPLEMENTATION

1. Set up visitations enough in advance to allow for teachers to fill out the Visitation Introduction Form. This is a one-time activity, and teachers do not need to fill out a new form for each subsequent visitation.
2. Two weeks prior to visitations, distribute, mail, or e-mail blank introduction forms to all visiting and host teachers and to the literacy coach from the other school. Also fill out one yourself.
3. Attach an example letter to the blank form to help teachers and coaches see what they might include in their own letters.
4. Instruct teachers to include information about their teaching background, as well as some preliminary information about their classes. This might include class size and brief information on the materials they use for literacy instruction.
5. Send the completed forms and the school brochure to the partner school at least one week prior to the first visitation.

PART 3

6. A few days before the visit, make sure that everyone has sent out their forms and that they have all been received by the partner school. Confer with teachers after they send or receive the introductory forms to gauge their expectations about observing and being observed.

7. As part of the introduction process, host schools can invite the visiting teachers and literacy coach to join them for a meeting before the observation. During this time, they can visit the classrooms when children are not present, talk briefly with the teachers about the information in their introductory letters, and have a chance to visit before the actual classroom observation. Although this may not be possible due to contractual issues, some schools have been able to pay their teachers a small stipend for this one-hour meeting prior to the observation.

REFLECTION, EVALUATION, AND PLANNING

1. What parts of the information on the letters seemed to be most helpful to teachers? Why?

2. In what ways did the Introductory Visitation Form help teachers feel more comfortable with each other and with the classroom observation? Should you add other items to the form?

3. After reading the introduction letters, how did teachers seem to adjust their thinking about the teachers they would visit or by whom they would be visited?

4. After the visitation is complete, debrief individually with teachers. What did teachers learn about the power of visitations? What were the positive and negative outcomes of a particular visit? What do you need to adjust for next time?

5. Did the observation sessions reveal a need for future professional development sessions?

Visitation Introduction Form

Please return this form to all visiting and host teachers and coaches by _____.

Name _____   ☐ Host Teacher   ☐ Visiting Teacher   ☐ Host Coach   ☐ Visiting Coach

School _____   School Year _____   Grade Level _____

Please use the space below to introduce yourself to the teachers and coach in your partner school. Choose any information helpful to start collaborating about each other's classroom practice. Include anything you value, such as strategies that seem to be working, materials or resources you're using, a personal learning goal, strategies you want to develop, or the needs of a particular group of children. See the example for one teacher's brief introduction to the teachers in her partner school.

Example Visitation Introduction Form

Please return this form to all visiting and host teachers and coaches by _March 9_____.

Name _Kellie Winston_____ ☐ Host Teacher ☒ Visiting Teacher ☐ Host Coach ☐ Visiting Coach

School _Gordon School_____ School Year _2006–2007_ Grade Level _K_____

Hi!

My name is Kellie Winston. I am the 2nd grade teacher at Gordon Elementary. This is my first year teaching in a public school system in America. I've taught 7th grade social studies and 3rd grade in Guadalajara, Mexico.

I student taught at Gordon School from September 2006 to November 2006. I did not think I would find a job so easily, but luckily enough, this 2nd grade position opened and I started on January 8, 2007.

I have 26 students in my class. Ten of those students are in the bilingual program. My room has both bilingual children as well as monolingual children. I am the only 2nd grade teacher at Gordon School.

I am excited to be part of this visitation program and excited to collaborate with other teachers. I feel as if I have not had enough training in guided reading and would like to see what a good guided-reading session looks like when I come to visit.

Many of my 2nd graders were reading at a 1st grade level when I first met them. There were a few students who were reading at about a 3rd grade level. As you can see, I have a variety of reading levels in my room! I would like to learn some good guided-reading strategies for each child to grow as a reader.

I look forward to meeting with you at your school next Monday!

Thanks,
Kellie

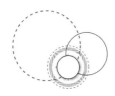

Using a Visitation Observation Form

TARGET
Elementary ✔   Middle School/High School ✔

Visiting teachers can be easily distracted by all there is to see during their first observation session in a host, or laboratory, classroom. Although the teachers and literacy coaches choose a focus before the observation is even scheduled, an unknown classroom holds the potential for many exciting things to examine. To help teachers make the most of their observation, the literacy coach can provide them with a Visiting Teacher Observation Form that is divided into student and teacher observation areas.

Teachers should have a general knowledge of the classroom they're visiting based on the information from the school brochure and the laboratory teacher's letter of introduction (see the "Sponsoring School Visitations" on page 212). One way to help teachers stay focused on the objective during observation time is to arrange for them to visit the classroom before the observation and when students aren't in the room. This gives visiting teachers complete freedom to look at displays, charts, student work, and other artifacts in the host's classroom.

During their observation, teachers can use the Visiting Teacher Observation Form to note what the laboratory teacher is doing and what students are doing and learning. They can also formulate questions as they arise during the observation. You may want to give examples of the kinds questions others have asked. For many teachers, this kind of observation is a novel experience. It is also important to give visitors examples of questions that are descriptive and nonevaluative.

The documentation from the Visiting Teacher Observation Form can serve as a springboard to start conversations between classroom teachers and coaches after the observation session is complete. However, the literacy coach remains invaluable in moderating the discussion, probing and prompting teachers to think deeply about what children did during the observation. To that end, coaches sometimes ask for copies of the documentation and questions to help them better lead future discussions.

PART 3

GOALS

- To make classroom visitations more productive for both the hosts and the visitors.
- To focus the visiting teachers' attention on teacher instruction and student learning.
- To provide a written format for visiting teachers to record their observations, comments, and questions about the observed lesson.
- To supply the kind of written notes that a visiting or host coach can use to lead the conversation among visiting and host teachers and coaches after the observation.

IMPLEMENTATION

1. Ideally, you and the partner coach and teachers can have a brief conversation before the observation begins. This can happen while the host teacher is getting students settled, or the coach can start class while the teacher meets with visitors to explain what they are going to see.
2. Ask the visiting teachers to record their observations of both teacher and student behaviors relative to the focus you've agreed on in advance. Explain that the completed form can help you organize the post-observation discussion.
3. Encourage visiting teachers to develop questions about the students' responses and the teacher's instruction and choices. These questions can be recorded on the form.
4. After the observation, encourage visiting teachers to share their comments. Ask teachers to explain their comments and help them realize the applications and importance of what they observed.
5. Ask permission to make copies of the visiting teachers' observation forms. Identify instructional behaviors and trends to support teacher reflection.

REFLECTION, EVALUATION, AND PLANNING

1. What was the nature of the teacher comments on the form?
2. How did the information on the form direct follow-up discussions? Do you need to modify the form to make it more effective?
3. Were there offensive comments on the sheet? Do you need to provide an example visitation form or talk about the importance of descriptive rather than evaluative comments? Did some teachers struggle to construct profitable questions? It may be necessary to construct a set of questions that could be used as templates.

PART 3

Visiting Teacher Observation Form

Date _____ Visiting Teacher _____ Grade Observed _____

Host Teacher _____ Host School _____

Lesson Focus _____

What I See Students Doing	What I See the Teacher Doing

My Questions:

Example Visiting Teacher Observation Form

Date __12/10/08__   Visiting Teacher __Sam Johnson__   Grade Observed __7__

Host Teacher __Susan Donaldson__   Host School __Hobson Middle School__

Lesson Focus __A comprehension strategy lesson about how to teach students to infer__

What I See Students Doing	What I See the Teacher Doing
• Seemed very interested in the story.	• Did a teacher think-aloud as she read a short story out loud and made inferences. Looked at ceiling when she made connection.
• Had trouble responding when teacher asked if they understood how her inferences helped her understand the story (on her last inference).	• After each inference, explained how it helped her understand what she was reading. I never saw anybody do that before. On last inference, asked students if they could figure out how it helped her understand story.
• Some students wrote their inferences on a piece of paper before sharing, others did not.	• Kept asking students whether they understood what she was doing.
• Room very quiet except for when they were sharing inferences.	• Did another read-aloud and took turns with students making inferences.
• Seemed very comfortable sharing . . . like this was an established routine to read and share.	• Asked students to turn to each other to share their inferences. Didn't ask them to explain how it helped them understand the story, though.

My Questions:

1. How do you decide where to stop and how many inferences?
2. Was there some direct instruction before you modeled in a think-aloud?
3. Why were they having so much trouble saying how the last inference helped you?
4. How does writing inferences down first help some of them but not others?
5. If they only share with each other, how do you know whether they're "getting it"?

Planning a Family Reading Night

TARGET

Elementary ✓   Middle School/High School __

Family reading nights are a wonderful opportunity to reinforce partnerships between schools and families. Because many schools do not allow students to attend this event without parents, family reading night becomes a unique opportunity to bring students, parents, and teachers together in a relaxed setting to celebrate and nurture a love of books. The responsibility of conceptualizing and organizing these events usually falls under the literacy coach's purview, and the Family Reading Night Checklist can help you coordinate the event.

A successful reading night has a variety of activities to engage parents and students at every grade level represented at the school. Activities can include any community resource that has the potential to support literacy. Along with highlighting school resources, you can invite community resources to set up information tables. Public libraries can send representatives with library card applications and flyers with information about library programs. Local bookstores can provide information about coming events and give away coupons. You can also ask a local bookstore to provide books as raffle prizes.

One popular activity that the literacy coach can plan is read-alouds for small groups of very young children led by teachers and older students. You can take advantage of times when children are engaged to talk to parents about encouraging their children to read or to show videos of engaging parent-child read-alouds.

Other activities for family reading night might include:

- **Flashlight Reading.** Students use flashlights to read books in a dark room.
- **Book 'n' Cook.** Read aloud a book that prominently features a food item, such as *The Giant Jam Sandwich,* by John Vernon Lord. Then make the item and eat it.
- **Guest Reader.** Ask local celebrities, such as news anchors or members of local sports teams, to read aloud.
- **Make 'n' Take Bookmarks.** Have precut blank bookmarks and markers available.
- **Crafty Books.** Have materials available so that students can complete simple projects from craft books.

ASCD   ☐ 221

- **Puppet Theater.** Set up and perform a familiar story. Supply paper bags, tongue depressors, and decorating supplies so that students can make their own puppets based on the story.
- **Book Character Bingo.** Create bingo cards with the faces of familiar book characters. Play bingo by answering questions about the character. For example, "He lives with the man in the yellow hat."
- **Reading and Writing Family Stories.** This session is held in the computer lab. Read aloud a book based on a family story, such as *Aunt Flossie's Hats (and Crab Cakes Later)*, by Elizabeth Fitzgerald Howard. Then have families write one of their family stories and share stories with the group.
- **Book Swap.** Invite participants to bring a book and take a book. You can save left-over books for the next family reading night.
- **Book Games.** Have board games based on books available.

The evening usually ends with a special culminating activity in the school auditorium and encouraging words from the principal. The overall goal is to encourage families to be mindful of and enhance their family reading practices.

GOALS

- To encourage excitement and celebration about the joys of reading.
- To highlight the important role family plays in developing young readers.
- To feature the literacy resources available in and out of the school.
- To celebrate the work of the teachers and students in the school's literacy program.

IMPLEMENTATION

1. Identify which group will help you develop, coordinate, and take responsibility for planning the event. A school literacy team (see "Creating a School Literacy Team" on page 181) would be a good option if you have one in place.
2. If the reading night is themed (this is optional), select a theme before you begin planning.
3. Clarify the budget. It is easier to work within a budget than to make cuts later.
4. If the budget allows, hire a storyteller or a drama troupe as a culminating event.
5. Contact the nearest public library and bookstore and ask for someone to sit at information tables. Ask the library for advice and the bookstore for donations.

6. Post a sign-up sheet with a list of possible room activities somewhere in the school. Include appropriate activities for all grade levels. Encourage teachers, administrators, support staff, paraprofessionals, and school volunteers to sign up.

7. Assign activities to specific rooms and acquire the necessary materials.

8. Make a schedule for the evening.

9. Design and send flyers home with the students, asking participants to enter through one door to ensure that no strangers enter the building and students are with parents and so that you can get an accurate count of the number of families that attend.

10. The day before the event, send reminders to all volunteers responsible for activities.

11. End the evening in the auditorium with your culminating event, being sure to publicly thank both attendees and volunteers. Follow with a simple snack, such as cider and cookies.

12. Send thank-you notes to all volunteers, the public library, and the bookstore.

13. Make notes that you or others can use to help plan future family reading nights.

REFLECTION, EVALUATION, AND PLANNING

1. Which of the evening's activities made the most explicit connections to reading? Which activities most carried the school's key messages about reading?

2. How many students attended? Did certain grade levels have larger showings? What can you do to attract families from grade levels that did not attend in adequate numbers?

3. Which activities were popular and which activities were not well received? Were activities that were less popular inappropriate for the grade levels or students they targeted?

4. Did any problems emerge during the evening? How can you avoid these problems in the future?

Family Reading Night Checklist

1. Form support committee.	
2. Select theme:	
3. Public library contact:	
4. Bookstore contact:	
5. Confirm budget amount: $	
6. Select culminating event performance or event:	
7. Post room activity sign-up sheet.	
8. Shop for supplies and materials.	
9. Contact local celebrity for guest reader.	
10. Make evening schedule.	
11. Write flyers.	
12. Send home flyers with parents—date:	
13. Send reminders to volunteers—date:	
14. Set up classrooms for activities.	
15. Set up tables for library and bookstore.	
16. Arrange to lock all doors except main entrance.	
17. Set out snacks.	
18. Evaluate room activities.	
19. Write thank-you notes to all volunteers.	
20. Create folder with notes for next year.	

PART 3

About the Authors

Shari Frost has been a classroom teacher, reading specialist, staff developer, and instructor at the university level. For more than 25 years, Frost taught K–5 in the Chicago Public Schools, and she was awarded the Golden Apple Award for Exemplary Teaching in 2000. Her classroom has been featured in instructional videos by the National Council of Teachers of English, Celebration Press, Scott Foresman, the State of Illinois, and the CTELL Project and in the Annenberg Teaching Reading K–2 video series. Frost has written articles in professional journals and magazines and chapters in professional books and is a regular columnist in *Choice Literacy,* an online publication.

Roberta Buhle has been a classroom teacher, a reading specialist, and a central office curriculum director in both suburban and urban schools. In addition to designing the Project Leap First Grade Literacy Intervention Program, she codeveloped a matching kindergarten intervention. She also helped design the Illinois Snapshots of Early Literacy, an assessment for K–2 early literacy. Buhle, who was named an Outstanding Educator by a local reading association, is a consultant to a state literacy center. She has written articles and chapters on early literacy and professional development.

Camille Blachowicz is professor of education and director of the Reading Program and Reading Center at National College of Education of National Louis-University. She has been a Fulbright fellow and received grants from the Spencer Foundation, the Chicago Community Trust, and the International Reading Association. Consulting nationally and internationally on vocabulary and reading instruction, Blachowicz was named to the roster of Outstanding Reading Educators by the International Reading Association. She is the author of seven books on literacy as well as numerous articles and chapters.

Currently, Frost, Buhle, and Blachowicz jointly direct the Literacy Coaching Institute at National College of Education of National-Louis University as well as the Literacy Partners Project, a collaboration between National-Louis University and the Chicago Public Schools to improve literacy in urban schools.

RELATED ASCD RESOURCES: LITERACY COACHING

At the time of publication, the following ASCD resources were available (ASCD stock numbers appear in parentheses). For up-to-date information about ASCD resources, go to www.ascd.org.

Books

Creating Dynamic Schools Through Mentoring, Coaching, and Collaboration by Judy F. Carr, Nancy Herman, and Douglas E. Harris (#103021)

Creating Literacy-Rich Schools for Adolescents by Gay Ivey, Douglas Fisher (#105142)

Differentiated Literacy Coaching: Scaffolding for Student and Teacher Success by Mary Catherine Moran (#107053)

The Fundamentals of Literacy Coaching by Amy Sandvold and Maelou Baxter (#107084)

Literacy Leadership for Grades 5–12 by Rosemarye Taylor and Valerie Doyle Collins (#103022)

Online Courses

Creating an Effective Secondary Reading Program by Tracy Wilson (#PD06OC57)

Six Research-Based Literacy Approaches for the Elementary Classroom by Kristen Nelson (#PD05OC53)

Networks

Visit the ASCD Web site (www.ascd.org) and click on Networks under About ASCD for information about professional educators who have formed groups around topics, including "Language, Literacy, and Literature." Look in the Network Directory for current facilitators' addresses and phone numbers.

For more information: send e-mail to member@ascd.org; call 1-800-933-2723 or 1-703-578-9600, press 1; send a fax to 1-703-575-5400; or write to Information Services, ASCD, 1703 N. Beauregard St., Alexandria, VA 22311-1714 USA.